"Khushbu Shah is showing a side of Indian food that everyone who enjoys eating should know about, and she does it in a way that makes it easy to understand and gets you excited to try it!"
JOSHUA WEISSMAN,
author of *An Unapologetic Cookbook*

"I can't begin to explain how stoked I am for *Amrikan*! It's packed with playful recipes like Rice Krispy Bhel, Crispy Paneer Burger, and Nutella Burfi. But more importantly, Khushbu Shah highlights how many of our immigrant mothers cook. By blending cultures and adapting to use what's accessible, they create new family recipes that are just as reflective of the diaspora as the foods they ate back home. Yes, please, to Carrot Halwa Sticky Buns!"
SOHLA EL-WAYLLY,
author of *Start Here*

"As one of the most exciting culinary voices of our generation, Khushbu Shah redefines what it means to be Indian American in her debut cookbook, *Amrikan*. Filled with emotion and recipes that demand your attention—this is a cookbook you will be returning to over and over for inspiration."
ANDY BARAGHANI,
author of *The Cook You Want to Be*

"I've been a fan of Khushbu Shah's work from day one, and her first cookbook knocks it out of the park, deeply wonderful and highly doable using mom-approved grocery store adaptations but also hella fun. I want to Julie–Julia the whole book."
DEB PERELMAN,
author of *Smitten Kitchen Keepers*

"Imagine being someone that has eaten at restaurants across the country, several times over, for your job! A discovered and informed perspective is apparent but what really drew me into Khushbu's inaugural cookbook were the craveable pathways of nostalgia and family tradition. Very little can compete with coming back home. Approachable, comfortable, and full of heart."
KRISTEN KISH,
chef, author, and host of *Top Chef*

"At last! You don't have to live in India and have access to only Indian ingredients to cook fantastic Indian food. The great Khushbu Shah has provided brilliant, original, easy, and, most of all, delicious Indian American recipes that will dazzle anyone's palate. You will want to make and eat every dish."
PHIL ROSENTHAL,
TV writer, producer, and
host of *Somebody Feed Phil*

"Like most Indian Americans of my generation, I grew up in a kitchen witnessing culinary genius: Mom. She never left the kitchen. If we went to restaurant, she'd eat spitefully, and then remark, 'I can make this at home. Why did we come here?' And then she would make it. But always with her own Indian twist. And then, as I grew older, I tried to imbue some of her styles into my own cooking and, every now and then, I actually made a winner. That's what this cookbook is: it's the best of every Indian Mom in this country mixed with the best of their kids. And now I'm going to cook every one of these dishes for my kids. Perhaps, like my mother, it can make me insufferable in restaurants. Thank you, Khushbu."
RAVI PATEL,
actor, director, producer

Amrikan

(Um-ree-kan)

W. W. NORTON & COMPANY
Independent Publishers Since 1923

Photography by Aubrie Pick

nrikan

125 Recipes from the Indian American Diaspora

KHUSHBU SHAH

Cover illustrations by We Are Out of Office
Cover design by Badal Patel, Super Spicy

Manufacturing by Toppan Leefung Pte. Ltd.
Book design by Badal Patel, Super Spicy
Text illustrations by We Are Out of Office
Art director: Allison Chi
Production manager: Devon Zahn

ISBN 978-1-324-03625-8

W. W. Norton & Company, Inc.
500 Fifth Avenue, New York, N.Y. 10110
www.wwnorton.com

W. W. Norton & Company Ltd.
15 Carlisle Street, London W1D 3BS

1 2 3 4 5 6 7 8 9 0

For every diaspora
kid with big dreams

Contents

Introduction

Amrikan (UM-ree-kan): a noun or adjective that Indians use to describe all things American. It's America, with a desi accent.

Peanut butter. Bisquick. Dinner rolls. Ketchup. While this list may read like a challenge basket on a high-stakes culinary competition show, each ingredient is actually a staple of the Indian American pantry. Come visit my parents' house any day of the week, and I guarantee you will find a sunshine-yellow box of Bisquick in the back right-hand corner of their pantry. Bisquick is a staple in our household not because we are rabid consumers of pancakes or biscuits, but because the baking mix serves as an integral part of my mom's Gulab Jamun recipe (page 285).

The beloved fried dessert, found on nearly every Indian restaurant menu in the West, is traditionally made with khoya (also known as mawa). Khoya requires boiling down milk for hours until it forms a soft, nutty dough. It's a time-consuming process, but premade khoya is readily available for purchase throughout India.

That's not quite the case in the United States. Indian immigrants quickly figured out, however, that if you combine Bisquick and dried milk powder, it offers a similar result, and you'll be able to make gulab jamun that are just as flavorful and tender—even though you're over 8,000 miles away from home.

That brings us to the main ingredient in the Indian American culinary lexicon: adaptation. Lack of access to staple Indian ingredients has led to clever adjustments, not limited to gulab jamun. Adaptation formed the baseline of mealtimes in my childhood household and in households similar to mine. It's the foundation upon which Indian cooking in America is built. A typical weeknight dinner at my house was often Pav Bhaji (page 203), one of Mumbai's most famous street foods. Traditionally it would be served with light and fluffy pav, Indian-style bread rolls (a relic of Portuguese colonization), but on a Thursday night after a long day of work, my mom would reach for a pack of dinner rolls, slice them in half, and generously butter each piece before toasting them in a pan.

For a light weekend lunch, she would grab a box of Cream of Wheat from the pantry and transform it into a comforting bowl of Upma (page 32), a thick, almost polenta-like dish that she always flavors with tomato and lots of fresh curry leaves. As I started to cook more, especially far away from my mom's well-stocked pantry, I realized that peanut butter (which I always had on hand) was an easy swap-in for the specific peanuts needed to make Cilantro-Mint Chutney (page 50), one of my favorite condiments of all time due to its versatility. Much of my cooking today is in this spirit: either adapting ingredients from my global pantry to work in Indian dishes or turning to the Indian pantry when cooking dishes from around the world.

But adaptation isn't a one-directional relationship where only Indian dishes are tweaked to accommodate American ingredients. Indians in America have also tweaked American foods with Indian flavors and spices to make them more palatable. Veggie burgers are beloved in my family, but I make them from a mixture of potatoes, sweet potatoes, black beans, and plenty of cumin, ginger, and Chaat Masala (page 63). Every hip Indian restaurant offers either "masala fries" or a riff on poutine (page 78), where the gravy is swapped for a tikka masala sauce or the cheese curds are replaced with paneer. And while some people keep hot sauce in their bag, many Indian Americans keep spice blends on hand when they travel—just in case.

As generations of immigrants and their children innovated with the ingredients and influences surrounding them, completely new dishes have emerged that are neither fully Indian nor fully American in their origins but delicious culinary innovations entirely unique to this diaspora. Take the Mango Pie (page 282), for example, made from canned mango pulp that jiggles in a buttery graham cracker crust. Or Indian pizza—invented in San Francisco in the 1980s—which is steadily gaining popularity (and to which I dedicate a whole chapter; see page 132).

Look, too, at Indian Tex-Mex: a cuisine people might not expect to exist, but you can find examples throughout Texas thanks to the state's large Indian American population.

While the Indian American culinary repertoire is expanding in exciting ways, the Indian American kitchen will always feature classic recipes that remain mostly untouched. These are the recipes that immigrants have doubled down on—the dishes that keep them connected to home and keep them whole. The pots of steaming, comforting Khichdi (page 206), a mix of lentils and rice that is cheap, filling, and nutritious. The Yogurt Rice (page 155), as simple in construction as in name. The bowls of spicy, steaming Sambar (page 131) that transport us through scent to the homeland, even as language and other customs start to fade. They are the dishes that feel embedded in our DNA. Meals that feel right when you eat them, that remind you that you are just as Indian as you are American. In a diaspora, adaptation also means finding ways to hold on.

The story of Indian food in America in many ways is the story of my family. I am the proud child of immigrants, and very much a product of this diaspora. But my family's story is just one piece of the puzzle. The food of the Indian American diaspora is some of the most exciting and accessible Indian cooking out there. It's a cuisine shaped by waves of immigration, resourceful home cooks, and generations determined to preserve their heritage while creating new traditions that honor their adopted homeland along the way. With this book, I hope to show you just how approachable, diverse, and—most importantly—*delicious* Indian food in America really is—even if you've never cooked it before.

Origin Story: Indian Food in America

You can't talk about Indian food in America without understanding the immigration patterns that shaped it. Though Indians have been in America since as early as the 1800s—including Sikhs who settled in California in the early 1900s, Bengalis who set up a thriving community in Harlem in the 1920s, and academics who attended American universities—it wasn't until the mid–1960s that Indians were able to really immigrate to America, previously restricted by a series of racist and nativist policies. When President Lyndon Johnson signed the Immigration and Nationality Act in 1965, it threw out the country-based quota system that for decades had favored immigrants from western Europe. A new system gave preference to skilled workers and opened up immigration from Asian countries like Korea—and India.

This first large wave of Indian immigrants arrived between the mid–1960s and the late 1970s, and the majority either had professional degrees or came to the United States to pursue them. Yes, a significant number were STEM professionals—hence the cliché that all Indians are doctors or engineers. These mostly white-collar workers were not interested in restaurant work as a career path, so only a few Indians opened food businesses.

The second wave of Indian immigrants, from the early 1980s through the mid–1990s, arrived through chain migration as family members of the first wave. Though many of these immigrants were also white-collar workers, there was a diversity of backgrounds and professions, and mom-and-pop-owned Indian restaurants started to dot the American landscape in major cities. These first two waves of immigrants were heavily from the Indian states of Punjab and Gujarat, so the foundation of Indian food in America is based largely on these regional cuisines, which are defined by having more wheat-based dishes like Simple Parathas (page 244), Masala Thepla (page 249), Simple Naan (page 255), and Puri (page 253) versus the cuisine of southern Indian states that feature more rice-based dishes like Basic Plain Dosas (page 121), Uttapam (page 129), and idli (steamed fermented rice cakes). Punjabi dishes like Classic Butter Chicken (page 188), Saag Paneer (page 215), and Dal Makhani (page 209) also tend to be the baseline of most Indian restaurant menus.

The third wave of Indian immigrants, or the IT generation, began arriving in the mid–1990s to work tech jobs. The resulting meteoric rise of immigrants hailed mainly from the southern Indian states of Tamil Nadu and Telangana. Today, it's estimated that 90 percent of H–1B visas, which are reserved for workers with a minimum of a bachelor's degree, are awarded to Indians. Google's campus now has an Indian canteen, and Apple provides several different Indian meal options daily. This wave of immigration was matched by a rapid increase in south Indian restaurants that opened to help feed a growing population.

My family arrived as part of the first wave of Indian immigration. My mom's oldest brother arrived in Syracuse, New York, in 1971, trading the 120-degree summers of Ahmedabad, Gujarat's largest city, for the frigid, sub-zero temperatures of upstate New York and a master's degree in engineering from Cornell. He eventually settled in Buffalo and, through the family visa system, was able to bring over his four siblings—including my mother. One of my uncles returned to India, but the others stayed. My parents, who met and married in their hometown of Ahmedabad, moved to yet another cold city: Detroit. My mom finished her dental degree while my dad completed his training as a doctor.

In Detroit, my parents rented a one-bedroom apartment that contained nothing more than a folding table, a sleeping bag, and a radio. It was here that my mom learned to cook. Like many, she learned to cook not out of passion, but rather necessity. She grew up as a staunch vegetarian in a Jain household, and her mom handled all the cooking. Detroit in the 1980s wasn't exactly a haven for vegetarians, and my mom did not trust restaurant food. Nor could she afford to not cook. She had a comfortably middle-class upbringing in India—an undeniable privilege that allowed her to afford a plane ticket to America in the first place. But that is about as far as her bank account extended.

She taught herself through a lot of trial and error, asking friends and relatives and consulting a couple of Gujarati cookbooks gifted to her to cook simple meals of dal and rice, or roti and vegetables. The first major Indian grocery store chain, Patel Brothers, opened in Chicago in 1974, but Indian groceries still weren't widely accessible even in the 1980s. Families would bring pantry staples in suitcases from India, but it wasn't exactly economical for my parents to fly back and forth between India and their new home just to grocery shop.

So, like many others in the American diaspora, my mom started adapting her favorite Indian dishes to work with the ingredients she could find. Members of the diaspora would learn from one another. In Detroit, their friends and colleagues were from all over the Indian subcontinent. Indian food became less staunchly regional through Indian American home cooking.

For centuries, before traveling became cheaper and the internet whizzed information across the country and around the world in a matter of sec-onds, food in India remained hyper-regional. For my mom, who grew up in Gujarat, Punjabi food was called "Western food," and something she had eaten maybe twice in her life. Same for south Indian sta-ples like crispy dosas and fried lentil fritters known as vada. Paneer, which many think of as a staple vegetarian protein, is something my mom, and many like her, learned to cook only once in the US. She had

never had Rajma (page 191), a beloved Punjabi dish of stewed kidney beans, until she immigrated, but it quickly became a regular part of her repertoire—as have south Indian classics like Uttapam (page 129) and Sambar (page 131).

So I and others like me, children of these early waves of Indian immigrants who were brought up in America, were raised on a steady diet of pan-Indian food. South Indian dishes like dosas were as frequent in my house as bowls of Gujarati Kadhi (page 217) spooned over rice. As we grew up, this repertoire has expanded to include "third-culture food," or dishes where American staples are effortlessly merged with Indian dishes and flavors.

Indian Food in America Today

I find it both fascinating and frustrating that Indian food remains misunderstood and relatively niche in the United States. There are nearly 4.8 million Indi-ans in the United States, but only 5,000 or so Indian restaurants according to 2020 estimates (the num-bers could now be lower, after the Covid–19 pan-demic hit the restaurant industry hard). Compare this to America's Thai population. There are around 340,000 Thais, but there are over 5,430 restaurants serving everything from papaya salads to plates of pad thai. Or compare this to another immigrant group with a similar population size: there are nearly 5 million Chinese Americans and well over 40,000 Chinese restaurants in America, or 8 times the num-ber of Indian restaurants.

Indians are one of the wealthiest and most suc-cessful immigrant communities in America. The authors of the book *The Other One Percent*, Sanjoy Chakravorty, Devesh Kapur, and Nirvikar Singh, offer a comparison between Native Americans and Indian Americans that starkly illustrates this fact. "A simple linguistic reversal—from American Indians to Indian Americans—reverses education and income [levels]."

The financial and educational success of Indians in America has failed to translate into a widespread understanding of Indian culture—especially its food.

While Chinese food has become a staple of mall food courts, Japanese food is sold in run-of-the-mill supermarkets across the country, and Mexican dishes like burritos and tacos have become as American as chicken nuggets and grilled cheese sandwiches, Indian food has yet to make it into the American dining lexicon beyond a handful of British curry house staples like butter chicken, samosas, and masala chai. (In the US, chai is often referred to as "chai tea," much to the chagrin of anyone of Indian origin. The phrase, beloved by chains like Starbucks, translates to "tea tea." Please don't use it.) In the past couple of years, a handful of other dishes, like khichdi and haldi doodh—aka turmeric milk aka "golden latte"—have started to float into the mainstream thanks to Goop acolytes and the growing Western obsession with Eastern medicine.

The relationship between Indian food in America is dramatically different from Indian food in Britain, where the British Indian invention of chicken tikka masala is the national dish, and "going for an Indian" is a regular Friday night activity. But America and India don't have the same level of direct, historical connection as the British, who colonized and pillaged India for centuries. (I guess the least they could do is appreciate Indian food!)

Though questions of why Indian food hasn't been as widely embraced as Thai or Japanese cuisine across the food delivery orders of America still lin-ger, I am happy to report there are several Indian American chefs now who are helping to translate and evangelize the cuisine. There is also a growing number of Indian American food brands selling products in stores like Whole Foods and Trader Joe's, and a handful of Indian Americans working in prominent positions in food media.

Still, these efforts only scratch the surface of the diversity of flavors, techniques, and excitements that India's vast regional cuisines offer. (It should be noted that the majority of this variety is not found in restaurants, but in Indian American home cooking, the largest source of inspiration for this book.) I can't wait for the day when Indian regional cooking is as understood and celebrated in America as the food of the regions of Italy and France.

YOUR FREEZER WILL SOON BE YOUR BEST FRIEND. LEARN MORE ON PAGE 17.

MYTH-BUS

Indian Food Is Only Curry

It's true that Indians eat curry, but we don't *only* eat curry. In fact, it's an incredibly small fraction of what we eat!

The origins of the word *curry* are murky to say the least, but many attribute it to a British bastardization of the Tamil word *kari*. Many Indians, especially Indian Americans, find the way the term is used in the West incredibly reductive. People will dismiss Indian food in its entirety by saying, "Oh, I don't like curry" or use the word in a derogatory manner, claiming that Indians "smell like curry."

This is not to say that "curry" doesn't exist in the Indian food vernacular, but it's different when Indians in India choose to keep or reclaim the term as a descriptor. There, the intent is not reductive, but simply another method of describing a cooking style like sabzi, shaak, fry, vindaloo, thoran, and so on. Egg Curry is very much real Indian food, and you will find two recipes for it in this book (pages 192 and 193).

This brings me to curry powder. Curry powder (or curry paste), which is a British invention, is not a standard inclusion in the Indian American pantry, nor is it regularly added to Indian dishes. Some Indians do use it—again, India and its diaspora is not a monolith—but unlike spices like turmeric, cumin, and mustard seeds, or spice blends like chaat masala and garam masala, curry powder is not commonly used. You can find it in exactly one recipe in this book, the Egg and Vegetable Kottu Parotta on page 37.

Indian Food Is Always Spicy

There is this wild misconception out there that Indians eat liquid fire, with a side of rice or naan. Just because Indian food is heavily spiced, that doesn't mean it is spicy. Seasoning your food gives it flavor, but not always heat!

There are 29 states in India, and each has its own distinctive style of cooking. While certain foods are, yes, incredibly hot, many dishes have little to no heat. Many savory Gujarati recipes call for a spoonful or two of sugar to balance the flavors, while dishes from places like Goa and Kerala use lots of coconut milk, and in the north you see the lasting influence of the Mughal empire, which preferred sweeter and subtler flavors like that of saffron. Also, as with any other cuisine in the world, the spice levels are frequently customizable, in this case by adding chutneys and spiced pickles to a dish.

TING

Indian Food Is Complicated

Do people really believe that Indians around the world, of which there are over a billion, somehow have more time to cook endlessly complex and intimidating dishes with only challenging ingredients? Indian food is just like any other cuisine in that once you have the basic pantry—which, yes, requires a decent number of spices (most of which are readily available in American grocery stores)—you can make a number of dishes in a short amount of time with ease. Just look at Italian food: lasagna is a dish with a fussy, multistep process, yet no one accuses Italian food of generally being "challenging" or "intimidating."

My mom, a dentist who runs her own practice and works full-time, often has only 20 or 30 minutes to throw together dinner. When I was growing up, she mainly cooked Indian food and always succeeded in having a complete hot and fresh meal on the table for the four of us. Yes, she is partially superhuman, but not necessarily in the kitchen. She just cooks many of the simple dishes that can be found in this book.

Indians, especially Indian Americans, also use several smart cheats and hacks to speed up cooking time. We buy ready-made spice mixes for common dishes so that we don't have to grind and mix spices each time we go to cook. We rely heavily on pressure cooking to quickly whip up meals, and we turn to soaking to reduce the cooking time of beans, lentils, and grains. We love quick dishes as much as we love spiced dishes. This is not to say there aren't recipes that we lovingly spend all day in the kitchen for, like Biryani Baked in a Squash (page 159). It's just not a daily thing.

ON SHARED BORDERS:
Why This Cookbook Is "Indian" and Not "South Asian"

I use the term "Indian" throughout this book very intentionally, but many of the dishes, ingredients, and techniques that I include belong equally to fellow members of the South Asian diaspora—particularly those from Pakistan and Bangladesh. The borders between the three countries didn't exist until 1947, when the British separated Pakistan from India, turning it into Pakistan and East Pakistan. It's a painful history known as Partition that tore apart families and resulted in a horror show that remains deeply nestled in the traumas the South Asian community carries today. East Pakistan, after the Bangladesh Liberation War, would transform into Bangladesh in 1971, with its own set of painful lingering traumas. And though politics demand the world put up physical borders between countries, it does not mean that foodways share those same borders.

Since these borders didn't exist until 73 years ago, there is an obvious overlap in the cuisines of these three countries in particular. Rasgulla is as Indian as it is Bangladeshi. Seekh kebabs are as Indian as they are Pakistani. Cooks from all three countries make great biryani. The three nations have an obsession with masala chai and mangoes, especially in the diaspora. And there is a shared affinity for the flavors of the "desh" or the homeland among those of my generation—the children of immigrants, raised oceans away in lands that are and aren't their own at the same time.

I am using "Indian" to simply narrow the scope of the book. The reality is that these pages manage to cover only a portion of the dishes that make up the foodways of the Indian American diaspora. Categorizing my recipes as anything but "Indian" would do a disservice to the equally vibrant and flavor-packed recipes of the Pakistani and Bangladeshi American diasporas (not to mention those of Sri Lanka, Nepal, and beyond). Each of these diasporas deserves their own cookbooks.

How to Use This Book

There's No Wrong Spice Level

Okay, I lied. There is one wrong spice level, and that is when a dish is so spicy that all you can taste is heat and zero flavor. Heat should enhance the flavor of a dish, not mask it. This was my goal when developing the recipes in this book: no recipe calls for pointless heat. Of course, everyone has a different tolerance for spice. There is nothing shameful about whatever your preference is. The spice levels I include in each recipe are merely suggestions and are easily adjustable. For most recipes in this book, heat is derived from two sources: green serrano peppers and Kashmiri red chili powder (or KRCP). If you prefer milder dishes, swap the serrano peppers for jalapeños (and make sure to remove the seeds), or reduce the amount of serrano pepper you use overall. As for the KRCP, which is made from milder chiles, simply use less of it. Do what makes your taste buds happy.

Don't Be Picky with Proteins

Just because a dish calls for one protein doesn't mean that you have to stick with it. The recipe might be called Classic Butter Chicken (page 188), but there is no reason that it wouldn't be as delicious if it was butter paneer, butter tofu, butter chickpeas, or even butter shrimp. If a recipe is made with paneer, it could easily be swapped out for mushrooms, chicken, pork, or your favorite seafood. Just make sure that whatever you decide to use, it is cooked all the way through or to the correct temperature. No getting sick while using this cookbook!

Embrace Your Freezer

What most people don't realize is how freezer-friendly Indian food can be. Made a pot of Dal Makhani (page 209)? You can freeze it. Whipped up Spinach Jeera Rice (page 152)? Throw it in the freezer. Cooked a batch of Makhani Mac and Cheese (page 162)? Freeze that, too. And, if the entirety of the recipe isn't suitable for the freezer, there's a good chance a component is (and I'll note as much in a recipe to help steer you). I always have containers of rajma, sambar, and several chutneys in my freezer at all times, plus a stack of frozen parathas, for quick and easy meals. I encourage you to make a double batch of dishes you love: eat half immediately and tuck away the rest in the freezer. Future so-hungry-you-don't-know-what-to-eat you will thank you.

Lean in to the Power of the Tadka

Tadka, which is also known as vaghar, chhonk, phodni, or several other names depending on where in India someone is from, is probably the most important and distinctive technique in Indian cooking. To make a tadka, you quickly bloom spices (and often aromatics like dried chiles and curry leaves) in hot fat, until they sizzle or pop or crisp up. It activates the aromas of these spices, which amps up the flavor of whatever dish it is being added to. A tadka can take a dish from being totally fine and completely forgettable to one of the most interesting and delicious things you've ever eaten. The tadka can serve as both a base flavor (added at the beginning of the recipe) or a finishing flavor (added at the end) for many dishes in this book. You can use any fat that you like (except butter, which has a high water content) to make a tadka. The most common fats used in this book are ghee, neutral oils like canola, and coconut oil.

Store-Bought Really Is Fine

In an ideal world, we would make every single thing from scratch: spice blends, beans, flatbreads, and more. But in the words of legendary Food Network host Ina Garten, "store-bought is fine" and, in fact, encouraged. Lots of Indian stores sell spice blends for every dish imaginable: butter chicken, pav bhaji, biryani, and many more. These are great if you don't want to stock your pantry with a glut of new spice jars (though the latter is more fun!). There's no shame in using these spice blends; Indian Americans use them all the time, and they are a glorious way to speed up the cooking process. Feel free to use canned beans when cooking from this book unless you are someone who enjoys making beans from scratch. And while I include plenty of flatbread recipes—from parathas to naan—there are incredible versions available in the freezer aisle of most Indian stores. I love the Kawan brand in particular for frozen parathas, which heat up quickly in a pan when you're ready to eat.

Buy a Pressure Cooker (It's worth it, I promise!)

While most of these recipes don't call for any special or fussy pieces of cooking equipment, the one thing worth purchasing if you don't already own one is a pressure cooker, ideally an electric model like the Instant Pot. The pressure cooker, introduced in 1959 to India, changed Indian cooking forever. It meant meat, beans, and lentils could all be cooked within minutes, rather than the hours it might take on the stovetop. If you're interested in making beans or lentils and Indian dishes on the regular, a pressure cooker is a worthy investment and makes recipes like Sambar (page 131), Spinach Tadka Dal (page 210), and Khichdi (page 206) a breeze to prepare.

ANY SALT IS GREAT

I might be picky about spices, but the idea that one salt is better than the other is a ridiculous concept to me. Salt is important to season your food, but use whatever salt you like and can find in stores, whether that is Diamond Crystal or Morton kosher salt or regular table salt. When developing recipes for this book I used plain Morton table salt, which is smaller in flake/crystal size than kosher salt. Therefore, if you prefer to use a kosher salt, you'll need to adjust how much salt is necessary for each dish by increasing the baseline amount. Everyone has a different preference for how salty they like their food, so make sure to taste as you go along and adjust as necessary. The only rule I have with salt is simple: don't forget to use it.

Please Please Please Invest in These Three Ingredients

There are only three items I will ask you to go out of your way to find simply because of how necessary they feel to the recipes—especially if you are interested in maximizing flavors.

KASHMIRI RED CHILI POWDER: If I were to take an educated guess, Kashmiri red chili powder is used in at least half the recipes in this book. The powder is made from dried and ground red chiles that have a vibrant red hue, and it has a fruity, sweet heat to it. While it might look like a more vibrant cayenne or paprika, it is less potent than the former and way spicier than the latter, so neither are great substitutes. (You can use either in a pinch, but remember to adjust the amount to reach the desired spice level.) KRCP adds not only heat to a dish, but also a lovely color. It's easy to source from any Indian store, but also excellent companies like Burlap & Barrel and Diaspora Co. that do thoughtful sourcing. Just keep in mind that KRCP can vary in heat level from brand to brand, so taste and use trial and error to get to your desired level of heat.

KASOORI METHI: While kasoori methi looks like something you might roll up and smoke, it's simply dried fenugreek leaves. I use it to add a certain *je ne se quoi* flavor to some dishes. You can't pinpoint exactly how it improves a dish, but there's no arguing that it does. It's a relatively affordable ingredient to keep on hand, readily available at any well-stocked Indian grocery store. And because it is dried, kasoori methi will last for a very long time before it starts to feel stale.

CURRY LEAVES: Curry leaves add a wonderfully savory note to any dish. Fresh curry leaves are ideal, as they have an incredible aroma that only amplifies when it hits any form of heat. You can often buy packs of fresh leaves from an Indian grocery store, and if those aren't available, check the freezer aisle for the frozen version. And if those are not available, dried curry leaves can be substituted in most recipes. The real move is to buy a curry leaf plant (it's the only plant I have!) and grow your own leaves to use whenever you'd like.

THE GRANDMA DISCLAIMER

And now for the standard disclaimer in every cultural cookbook: Please remember that these are not your mom's or your grandma's recipes. I am sure they are great cooks and their version of whatever dish is amazing and wonderful. I highly encourage you to write them down and share them with the world, too! The recipes in this book are just one method for making a dish, and it could be dramatically different from how your family makes it. That does not make my version incorrect, nor does it make your family's version incorrect. All food, made with care (and enough spices and salt), is delicious.

The Amrikan Pantry

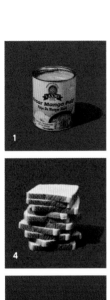

1 CANNED MANGO PULP

2 SEV

3 RICE KRISPIES CEREAL

4 WHITE SANDWICH BREAD

5 MAGGI NOODLES

6 URAD DAL (SKIN OFF)

7 PEANUT BUTTER

8 BASMATI RICE

9 KASOORI METHI

10 GHEE

11 MILK POWDER

12 DRIED RED CHILIES

13 TOMATO PASTE

14 KETCHUP

15 GARLIC

16 LONG-GRAIN WHITE RICE

17 JAGGERY

18 CURRY LEAVES

19

20

21

22

23

24

25

26

27

28

29

30

31

32

33

  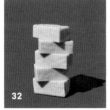

34

35

36

37

38

39

19 URAD DAL (SKIN ON)

20 CANNED DICED TOMATOES

21 CILANTRO

22 CHICKPEAS

23 MOONG DAL

24 PICKLED JALAPEÑOS

25 SERRANO PEPPERS

26 GINGER PASTE

27 COCONUT OIL

28 CONDENSED MILK

29 BISQUICK

30 CANDIED FENNEL SEEDS

31 BESAN (GRAM FLOUR)

32 PANEER

33 GINGER

34 MINT

35 KIDNEY BEANS

36 GARLIC PASTE

37 COCONUT MILK

38 YOGURT

39 A FLOWER FOR YOU

BREA

I've never agreed with the idea that you can only eat certain foods at certain times of the day. Soup is wonderful at 9 a.m. and at 9 p.m., dough-nuts are just as fun at noon as they are at 6 p.m., and rice can be consumed at all hours. Basically, anything can be breakfast if you believe in it enough.

KFAST

Masala Shakshuka

1 tablespoon olive oil

½ large white onion, diced

½ red bell pepper, diced

½ green serrano pepper, minced

2 tablespoons garlic paste
 or 6 garlic cloves, minced

1 tablespoon ginger paste or 1-inch
 piece fresh ginger, grated

1 teaspoon Garam Masala (page 62)

1 teaspoon salt

½ teaspoon ground black pepper

½ teaspoon ground cumin

½ teaspoon ground coriander

½ teaspoon Kashmiri red chili powder

¼ teaspoon ground turmeric

1 (14½-ounce) can diced tomatoes

3 tablespoons whole milk

¼ to ½ cup water (if needed)

4 large eggs

½ cup crumbled feta

Chopped fresh cilantro, for garnish

❄ FREEZER NOTE

You can absolutely freeze the tomato gravy base (stop before you crack in the eggs) in an airtight container for 3 months. Reheat in a skillet until heated through and then continue the recipe from there. I love the idea of freezing a half batch of the base for a quick future meal.

I don't know if it is the Indian auntie within me, but I move through the world noticing just how many dishes are *almost* Indian food, but aren't *technically* Indian food. The best example of this? Shakshuka, the insanely popular North African/Middle Eastern dish of jammy tomatoes and yolky eggs. The first time I ate it, I realized this is basically tomato-onion gravy—or cooked-down tomatoes and onions—which is the base of so many north Indian dishes, plus some eggs baked on top.

Shakshuka is incredibly versatile and easily adapts to whichever flavors you might want. To make it more Indian, I throw in spices like garam masala, cumin, and coriander. I like to serve shakshuka with naan, which feels like a distant relative of pita. (It is also great with the Tadka Focaccia on page 258.) You could add some crumbled paneer on top of the dish before baking to make it even more Indian, but I prefer to use feta, which offers a nice burst of saltiness.

In a large skillet, heat the oil over medium-high heat. Add the onion and bell pepper and sauté for 4 to 6 minutes, until soft and tender, then add the serrano pepper, garlic, and ginger and give it a good mix. Allow the mixture to cook for another minute, then add the garam masala, salt, pepper, cumin, coriander, chili powder, and turmeric. Stir to make sure the spices evenly coat the vegetables, then add the tomatoes with their juices to the pan. Let the mixture simmer for 10 minutes so that all the flavors meld. Stir in the milk to make the gravy more silky. If the sauce is too thick and jammy at this point, add a little water and let it simmer for another 2 to 4 minutes.

Use a spoon to carve out four wells in the tomato mixture and crack an egg into each. Sprinkle the feta around the pan. Cover the pan and cook until the egg whites set but the yolk remains runny, 2 to 3 minutes. Scatter cilantro over the top and serve.

Saag Paneer Frittata

6 large eggs

1½ cups Saag Paneer (page 215)

¼ cup chopped scallions

Salt and ground black pepper to taste

1 tablespoon olive oil or ghee

¼ cup crumbled feta

◉ **SERVING NOTE**

The frittata is also satisfying straight out of the fridge, stuffed between two pieces of toast to make a quick sandwich.

🥣 **STORAGE NOTE**

Frittatas don't freeze well, but leftovers will keep, well covered, for a few days in the fridge.

I am a huge fan of frittatas because of how unfussy they are to make and how easy they are to eat. This one is a speedy way to use up saag paneer leftovers. I like to add some feta on top because there is never enough paneer in leftover saag paneer and all frittatas could benefit from more cheese. Just remember, even though this is in the "breakfast" chapter, this frittata is a great lunch, dinner, or snack too.

Preheat the oven to 375 degrees F.

In a medium bowl, whisk together the eggs until there are no streaks. Fold in the saag paneer and scallions and season with salt and pepper. Mix until well combined. The eggs will turn a pale green color (the *Green Eggs and Ham* vibes are intentional!).

Heat the oil in a large oven-safe cast-iron or nonstick skillet over low heat. Add the egg mixture and scatter the crumbled feta evenly on top. Transfer to the oven and bake until the eggs are set and don't jiggle when you shake the pan, 20 to 25 minutes. Let the frittata cool slightly, then cut into wedges and serve.

Saffron Chia Seed Pudding

10 to 15 saffron threads

1 (14-ounce) can full-fat or
light coconut milk

6 tablespoons chia seeds

2 tablespoons maple syrup

1 teaspoon vanilla extract

¼ teaspoon ground cardamom

Pinch salt

2 tablespoons ground pistachios (optional)

Fresh, frozen, or dried fruit of
choice, for topping (optional)

🍲 STORAGE NOTE

This recipe doesn't freeze well, but the pudding (when not topped with fruit) stays well in an airtight container in the fridge for up to 5 days.

Saffron is supposed to have a whole Avengers-style range of health benefits. It's allegedly a powerful antioxidant, high in nutrients like vitamin C, and a mood booster. I can attest only to that last benefit, simply because I love the nuanced floral flavors of good saffron, and the charming golden hue it gives everything it touches.

On a quest for breakfast ideas that weren't pancakes, scrambled eggs, oatmeal, avocado toast, or yogurt topped with fruit, I started making chia seed pudding. I love the slithery, bouncy texture chia seeds develop after they soak in liquid, but I found myself bored of the typical flavors—the usual cycle of vanilla, chocolate, or more vanilla.

So I decided to make a version modeled after one of my favorite desserts: Shrikhand (page 291). I added saffron, cardamom, and ground pistachios because of the way they mimic the flavors of shrikhand, and swapped out my usual almond milk for coconut milk because of the richness it adds to the bowl. I sweeten this pudding gently with maple syrup, but you can use honey or another sweetener. I like to top it all off with a handful of diced apples, banana slices, or chunks of mango if they are in season.

Put the saffron in a small bowl and microwave for 10 to 15 seconds. This dries out the saffron, and you should then be able to crumble it into a fine powder with your fingers. Transfer the powdered saffron to a medium bowl and add the coconut milk, chia seeds, maple syrup, vanilla, cardamom, and salt. Give everything a good stir, then scoop into 4 single-serving containers or one large jar. Cover and let the pudding firm up in the fridge overnight, shaking the jar(s) after 1 hour in the fridge so that the chia seeds don't clump. When ready to serve, layer with pistachios and fruit as desired.

Shahi Tukda French Toast

1 tablespoon unsalted butter

10 saffron threads

2 ½ cups whole milk, divided

½ cup heavy cream

6 large eggs

⅓ cup brown sugar

1 tablespoon vanilla extract

1 teaspoon salt

1 ½ teaspoons ground cardamom

1 (1-pound) brioche loaf, cut into 10 slices

Condensed milk, for garnish

Crushed pistachios, for garnish

Rose petals, for garnish (optional)

🌿 INGREDIENT NOTE

You can substitute milk for the cream, but cream makes the dish feel super rich and you deserve great things.

It feels like every write-up about shahi tukda is the same. People always mention that the dessert's origins can be traced back to the 1600s during the Mughal rule of modern-day India. That it was a dish created for and fed to royals. That the name literally translates to "royal piece" or "royal bite." That shahi tukda is often described as "Indian bread pudding." And all of that is true, except for the fact that I've always felt the dish has more French toast vibes than bread pudding vibes—and so I transformed it into just that.

The traditional recipe calls for frying thin pieces of white bread in ghee, then soaking them in a sugar syrup and drowning the fried bread in a custardy sauce of cooked-down milk, sugar, and saffron, and garnishing with nuts like pistachios. Delicious, but more work than I want it to be. Instead of having to patiently watch milk thicken, you make a simple custard amped up with saffron, vanilla, and cardamom to soak the bread in, and drizzle the final product with sweetened condensed milk. You want to make sure to use a properly soft white bread, like brioche or challah. This dish is easy to make for a group and can be prepped the night before. Be sure to garnish the French toast with a generous amount of pistachios and edible rose petals, if you can. If you have any edible gold or silver foil on hand, use it, too—this is a dish for royals, after all.

Recipe continues

Butter a 9 x 13-inch baking dish and set aside.

In a small microwave-safe bowl, crush the saffron between your fingers. Add 1 tablespoon milk and microwave for 15 seconds, then give the milk a swirl. The saffron should infuse the milk and turn it a beautiful yellow. Pour the saffron-infused milk into a larger bowl, add the rest of the milk, and stir to combine. Add the cream, eggs, brown sugar, vanilla, salt, and cardamom and give it a good whisk until the mixture is well combined. Thoroughly soak each slice of bread in the milk mixture, then layer the slices like shingles in the buttered pan. Pour any leftover custard evenly over the bread. Cover and refrigerate overnight (though you can bake right away if you want).

Preheat the oven to 350 degrees F.

Bake the French toast, uncovered, for 45 minutes, or until the bread is lightly golden and toasty. Drizzle with condensed milk and garnish with crushed pistachios and edible rose petals, if using. It's definitely more fun with all the garnishes.

Upma

2 tablespoons neutral oil

1½ teaspoons cumin seeds

1½ tablespoons urad dal (black gram)

2 tablespoons chopped raw
    cashews (optional)

20 fresh curry leaves (see Ingredient Note)

1 cup semolina flour (see Ingredient Note)

1 green serrano pepper, minced

3 cups water

1 small tomato, diced

2 tablespoons full-fat yogurt, plus
    more for serving (optional)

Salt to taste

❧ INGREDIENT NOTE

If you cannot find fresh curry leaves, you
can use dried curry leaves after soaking
them in water for 10 minutes to rehydrate
them. If you cannot find semolina, Cream
of Wheat is a good substitute, but often,
semolina (also known as sooji) is typically
the more affordable option and can be
readily found at most Indian grocery stores.

❄ FREEZER NOTE

Upma can be frozen in an airtight container for up to 2 months. Reheat with
a splash of water in the microwave to
freshen it up. The texture is best the day
you make it, though.

In my version of the children's book *Goldilocks and the Three Bears*, this upma recipe is the porridge that is "just right." Made from a base of thickened semolina flour, upma is beloved all over India and in the diaspora. It is an extremely popular breakfast, especially accompanied by a cup of masala chai. When I was growing up, upma was always a lazy Sunday lunch, alongside a plate of freshly cut fruit. Now that I'm an adult, it has become a go-to dinner when I want comfort food. Upma is slightly thicker in texture than polenta but just as creamy, thanks to the addition of a few tablespoons of yogurt. Cashews are optional, but they add a welcome crunch.

First, make the tadka, which will cook quite quickly. Heat the oil in a medium saucepan over medium heat until it glistens. Add the cumin seeds to the hot oil and watch them sizzle, about 2 seconds. Then add the urad dal and chopped cashews, if using. Stir the tadka for a minute, until the cashews are toasted.

Turn the heat down to medium and stir in the curry leaves, sem-olina flour, and serrano pepper. Stir until the semolina starts to brown and smell nutty, 4 to 5 minutes. Add the water, tomato, yogurt, and salt but don't stir, as it will cause clumping.

Cover, turn the heat down to low, and let the upma cook for 4 to 5 minutes, until thickened and all the water is absorbed. Uncover, turn the heat up to medium, and stir constantly for 2 minutes to thicken. Turn off the heat, cover, and let sit for 5 minutes. Serve the upma on its own, with a cup of chai, or with additional plain yogurt on the side.

Ultimate Desi Egg Sandwich

2 large eggs

1 tablespoon milk

¼ small red onion, finely diced

1 tablespoon finely chopped fresh cilantro

⅓ green serrano pepper, minced

¼ teaspoon Chaat Masala (page 63)

¼ teaspoon salt

¼ teaspoon ground black pepper

1 tablespoon unsalted butter

2 slices bread of your choice

2 slices melty cheese, such as provolone

Ketchup or Spicy Cilantro Chutney
    (page 51), for serving

I didn't grow up eating egg sandwiches, but after over a decade of living in New York City, a bodega-style egg-and-cheese practically became a religion, especially on busy weekday mornings. When I had more time, I liked to make my eggs at home where, more often than not, I would whip up a batch of akuri, or Indian-style scrambled eggs cooked with onions and chiles. It's a dish that originates in the Parsi community and one of the best egg dishes out there. This egg sandwich is where the two dishes meet: there's the gooey, melted cheese, a signature of the bodega classic, while the eggs are spiced the way I would do it for a plate of akuri. The folding technique is quite simple once you practice it once or twice. I learned it from a YouTube video on Indian bread omelets, a popular street food especially at train stations. I love this neat and tidy sandwich for break-fast with a side of fresh fruit, but the sandwich also makes for a great solo diner.

In a small bowl, beat the eggs. Add the milk, onion, cilantro, ser-rano pepper, chaat masala, salt, and black pepper and mix well.

Melt the butter in a large nonstick skillet over medium heat. Add the egg mixture and make sure it spreads evenly across the pan. Working quickly, press one bread slice onto the egg so the egg coats that side of the bread, then flip it over and place it on the right half of the eggs. Repeat with the second slice of bread, placing it on the left half—make sure the 2 slices are lined up and facing the same way. Let the eggs cook for about 2 minutes, until set.

Recipe continues

❄ FREEZER NOTE
You cannot freeze this sandwich.

Using a wide spatula, carefully flip the entire omelet over so that the bread is now on the pan and the egg layer is facing up. Add 1 slice of cheese to each half of the eggs and let it cook for about 1 minute, then fold any egg that is hanging off the slices of bread toward the center. Fold the left slice of bread over so that it sits on top of the right slice of bread to form a sandwich. Flip the sandwich and continue to cook until both sides are golden brown. Cut the sandwich in half and serve with ketchup or green chutney for dipping.

Egg and Vegetable Kottu Parotta

4 Super Flaky Parathas (page 247) or store-bought frozen parathas (see Ingredient Note on page 29)

3 tablespoons neutral oil, divided

1 teaspoon black mustard seeds

1 teaspoon fennel seeds

Handful fresh curry leaves (optional)

1 medium white onion, diced

1 medium leek, chopped

2 scallions, chopped

1 green serrano pepper, minced

1 tablespoon garlic paste *or* 3 garlic cloves, minced

1½ teaspoons ginger paste *or* ½-inch piece fresh ginger, grated

2 teaspoons Kashmiri red chili powder

1 teaspoon curry powder

1 teaspoon ground coriander

½ teaspoon ground turmeric

2 Roma tomatoes, diced

1 teaspoon salt

2 large eggs

½ carrot, shredded

Handful fresh cilantro, for garnish (optional)

South Asians are excellent at stir-frying not only vegetables and rice, but also bread. Enter kottu parotta (also known as kottu roti—kottu translates to "chopped" or "minced"), a street food that is popular in Sri Lanka and the state of Tamil Nadu in India. It makes quick work of leftover parathas by chopping them up and cooking them with a pile of scrambled eggs, vegetables, and a fistful of spices. The flakier the paratha, the tastier this is.

There are small differences between the Sri Lankan version and the Indian version of this dish, namely that the former uses a dark roasted Sri Lankan curry powder, versus this recipe which calls for regular curry powder (the only time you will find curry powder in this book). The Sri Lankan version also traditionally uses godamba roti as the base, which is paper thin. I like to use parathas, which are a bit thicker. Both versions are frequently served with chicken curry, or just the gravy portion from that curry, which is also known as a salna. To keep this vegetarian-friendly and to streamline the recipe, there is no side gravy, but feel free to make one if you'd like.

This recipe is extremely customizable. Feel free to add more eggs or any vegetables of your choosing (bell peppers work particularly well). If it's too spicy or not spicy enough, play with the heat levels. Folding in some shredded cheese is also delicious. I sometimes sprinkle on feta, regardless of how nontraditional that is, because feta is the best.

If using frozen parathas, heat them according to the package instructions. Cut the parathas into strips about 2 inches long and ½ inch thick and set aside.

Recipe continues

If you don't feel like making the parathas, there are great frozen options out there. I like the Malabari Paratha from Trader Joe's or the Flaky Paratha by Kawan, which is available in most Indian stores.

This does not freeze well but leftovers will keep in the fridge for 2 to 3 days.

Heat 2 tablespoons oil in a large, heavy-bottomed skillet over medium-high heat. Add the mustard and fennel seeds and let them pop and splutter for 10 to 15 seconds. Add the curry leaves, if using, and let them frizzle for another 20 seconds. Add the onion, leek, scallions, and serrano pepper and sauté until the onion and leek soften, about 4 minutes. Stir in the garlic and ginger, then add the chili powder, curry powder, coriander, and turmeric and let it cook for 20 to 30 seconds. Add the tomatoes and salt and cook, stirring constantly, until the tomatoes are somewhere between mushy and jammy, 3 to 4 minutes. Push the mixture to the side.

In a small bowl, whisk the eggs. Add the remaining 1 tablespoon oil to the pan, then pour the eggs into the empty space in the pan. Let cook for 15 seconds, then scramble the eggs into the tomato mixture. Add the shredded carrot and paratha strips and stir to combine well. You want each piece of paratha to be coated. Remove from the heat and garnish with cilantro, if you like.

Maggi Omelet

2 (2.46–ounce) packets Maggi
   Masala 2–Minute Noodles

3 large eggs

4 scallions, chopped

¼ red onion, diced

⅓ cup crumbled feta

Ground black pepper to taste

Butter, for frying

Ketchup, for serving

🌿 INGREDIENT NOTE

You can find Maggi noodles at most Indian grocery stores or online, and you might want to buy a few extra packets to eat solo—they are the best instant ramen, if you ask me.

In 2015, I was a baby journalist with my first proper food writing job at Eater, where I was asked to write a blog post about chef David Chang's latest antic: the Ramlet. In a video for the now-defunct food magazine *Lucky Peach* (RIP), Chang simply added two packets of instant ramen seasoning to three eggs, whisked it all up with chopsticks, and cooked it into a silky French-style omelet. The recipe has remained firmly lodged in my brain for all these years, and I have always admired the high-brow/low-brow structure of the recipe.

I have since found myself thinking about the Ramlet often, not because of what Chang did, but because of what he wasn't brave enough to do. To leave the ramen noodles out from the recipe was a giant miss in the texture department! There is a genius Italian dish called frittata di spaghetti that uses a couple of eggs and a bit of cheese to bind together a tangle of leftover pasta, transforming it into a crispy-but-chewy savory pasta cake.

This omelet sits in the middle of the Venn diagram of the Ramlet and a frittata di spaghetti, replacing the standard Asian instant ramen seasoning with the packets from Maggi noodles (India's beloved version of instant ramen). My recipe, most importantly, includes the noodles too! Plus some feta cheese and onions for salt and sharpness.

Recipe continues

Bring a medium saucepan of water to a boil over medium-high heat. Add the noodles, setting aside the seasoning packets, and cook until al dente, 3 to 4 minutes. Drain.

In a medium bowl, whisk the eggs. Add the reserved seasoning packets, scallions, red onion, and feta and mix thoroughly. Add the cooked noodles, along with some freshly cracked black pepper, and give it a good stir.

Melt a generous knob of butter in a medium nonstick skillet over medium heat. Pour the egg and noodle mixture into the pan and let it cook, undisturbed, for 4 to 5 minutes, until the bottom is set and gently browned. Place a plate over the pan and flip the cooked side onto the plate. Melt a little more butter in the pan, then slide the uncooked side of the omelet back into the pan. Let it cook for another 3 minutes, or until golden and set. Slide the omelet out of the pan and cut into wedges. Honestly, this tastes best with ketchup—no shame!

Carrot Halwa Sticky Buns

DOUGH

3 tablespoons unsalted butter

1 cup full-fat or 2% milk

4 tablespoons granulated sugar, divided

1 (¼-ounce) envelope active dry yeast
(2¼ teaspoons)

3 cups all-purpose flour, plus
more for dusting

Olive oil, for greasing

FILLING

1 pound carrots, peeled and
grated (about 5 cups)

1½ (12-ounce) cans evaporated milk

¼ teaspoon ground cardamom

¼ cup condensed milk

¼ cup brown sugar

1 tablespoon unsalted butter or ghee,
melted, plus more for greasing

⅛ teaspoon ground nutmeg

Pinch salt

¼ cup sliced pistachios (optional)

Milk, for brushing

FROSTING

1 cup condensed milk

8 ounces cream cheese, at room temperature

½ teaspoon ground cardamom

Sliced pistachios, for garnish (optional)

I always thought Cinnabon was the pinnacle of American mall food court dining, with its giant, gooey, almost-the-size-of-your-face cinnamon rolls and its signature cinnamon-sugar scent's ability to come find you no matter where in the mall you were. Ever since my first bite, I was hooked, and have had a soft spot for fluffy cinnamon rolls ever since. So you can imagine how excited I was when I saw my friend Farhan Momin making a version filled with carrot halwa on his Instagram stories.

Leave it to Farhan to come up with the brilliant idea to swap cinnamon, sugar, and butter for a spread made with halwa, a beloved dessert made by patiently cooking down grated carrots with milk, sugar, and spices. But Farhan has always been a bit of an overachiever: not only is he an incredibly talented cook (and former *MasterChef* contestant) who runs Farmo Cooks, a super creative pop-up where he makes things like chapli kebab patty melts, he is also a full-blown dentist.

This recipe is inspired by Farhan's ingenuity and is worth the endurance it requires to cook down the carrots until they turn into a gorgeous, spreadable filling. You can easily make the carrot halwa filling and the cardamom cream cheese frosting ahead of time so that assembly moves quickly—and you can get to the eating part faster. If you want to impress guests, this is the dish to make.

First, make the dough. In a medium saucepan, melt the butter over low heat. Add the milk and 1 tablespoon granulated sugar. Once the milk hits 110 degrees F, or lukewarm to the touch, take the pan off the heat (you don't want it to be hotter than this, because it will kill the yeast). Add the yeast and let it bloom. It should look a little foamy after 10 minutes; if it's not, it means your yeast is dead and you need to get fresh yeast and start over. Pour the mixture into a medium bowl, add the remaining 3 tablespoons granulated sugar, and let it dissolve completely.

Recipe continues

MY PASTRY-
OBSESSED NIECES!

Add the flour, 1 cup at a time, and stir with a wooden spoon until a shaggy dough forms. It will be sticky! Knead with your hands (or a stand mixer with a dough hook) for about 10 minutes, until the dough is smooth and quite elastic. It will no longer be sticky at this point. Remove the dough and lightly grease the bowl with olive oil. Form the dough into a ball, return it to the bowl, and cover the bowl with plastic wrap or a lid. Place it somewhere warm for 1 hour. It should double in size.

While the dough is rising, make the carrot halwa. Combine the grated carrots, evaporated milk, and cardamom in a medium saucepan. Bring to a simmer over medium heat, then let the mixture cook down and thicken, stirring occasionally to avoid burning, 40 to 45 minutes. Add the condensed milk, brown sugar, melted butter, nutmeg, and salt. Mix until well combined, then cook down the halwa for another couple of minutes. Set aside to cool to room temperature.

Butter a 9 x 13–inch baking pan. Once the dough has doubled in size, roll it out on a lightly floured surface to an 11 x 14–inch rectangle, with the long sides parallel to the edge of work surface. Spread the cooled carrot halwa in an even layer over the dough, leaving 1 inch of dough uncovered at the top of the rectangle. Scatter the pistachios on top, if using. Starting from the side closest to you, roll the dough into a tight spiral, ending at the strip of uncovered dough. Cut into 12 pieces using either unflavored dental floss or a sharp chef's knife. Place the rolls cut side down in the prepared baking pan, cover with plastic wrap or a clean kitchen towel, and let them proof in a warm spot in your kitchen for 20 to 30 minutes.

Preheat the oven to 375 degrees F.

Brush the rolls with a thin layer of milk and bake for 20 to 25 minutes, until lightly golden brown.

While the rolls are baking, make the frosting. In a small bowl, combine the condensed milk, cream cheese, and cardamom and mix with a lot of arm muscle, a hand mixer, or a stand mixer until fluffy and even.

Spread the frosting on the buns while still hot and scatter more sliced pistachios on top, if using.

Moong Dal Waffles

1 cup skinless moong dal, soaked in
water overnight and drained

1 green serrano pepper, minced

2 tablespoons kasoori methi (optional)

1 tablespoon ginger paste *or* 1-inch
piece fresh ginger, grated

1 tablespoon garlic paste
or 3 garlic cloves, minced

1 tablespoon besan flour

1½ teaspoons salt

Neutral oil, for greasing

🌿 INGREDIENT NOTE

Moong dal is also known as split mung beans. It's very important to use the skinless version in this recipe to achieve the proper texture. You can use a different skinless lentil of your choice, but moong dal offers the lightest and crispiest result.

❄ FREEZER NOTE

The cooked waffles freeze well in an airtight container for up to 1 month. To reheat, thaw and then place in a toaster.

What is the point of owning a waffle maker if you aren't going to try to waffle basically everything in your kitchen at some point? I've had many successes—hash browns, falafel mix, even frozen mozzarella sticks—they all cook nicely in a waffle maker. But my favorite use for my waffle maker might be to make lentils crispy without frying them. Enter these moong dal waffles. The batter is way less work than a traditional or Belgian waffle batter: you blitz soaked lentils with garlic, ginger, and serrano pepper for a bit of a kick, and cook this batter until it develops a super crispy exterior and fluffy interior. Then top it as you please with Spicy Cilantro Chutney (page 51), ketchup, and maybe even a fried egg. It's a recipe that is gluten-free, dairy-free, and vegan, but most definitely packed with flavor.

Combine all of the ingredients in a food processor or blender and process the mixture until it forms a thick paste, adding a little water if needed. Run the food processor for another minute or two until the batter starts to become frothy.

Heat a waffle pan on high and oil it well.

Pour in the recommended amount of batter per your waffle machine's instructions and cook until the waffles are cooked through and crispy, usually 5 to 8 minutes. Serve with your favorite toppings.

Chutneys, raitas, and masala blends are what take Indian dishes to the next level, or what help transform non-Indian dishes into something that tastes desi. Seriously, add a bit of Chaat Masala (page 63) or Garam Masala (page 62) to basically anything and it will taste instantly Indian.

CHUTNEY, RA

ITAS & MORE

Cilantro-Mint Chutney

1 bunch cilantro (leaves and stems)

⅓ bunch mint (leaves and stems)

1½ green serrano peppers

3 tablespoons lemon juice

1 tablespoon natural unsalted peanut
   butter *or* 3 tablespoons roasted peanuts

1½ tablespoons sugar

1 teaspoon salt

❄ FREEZER NOTE

This freezes incredibly well. I use half a batch immediately and freeze the other half in an airtight container. Let it thaw in the fridge or on the counter before using.

This chutney is one of the most versatile condiments in the Indian recipe canon. I like to keep a jar in my freezer so that I am always prepared. Cilantro-mint chutney is wonderful for dunking samosas (pages 114 to 120), spreading on sandwiches (like the Bombay Grill Sandwich, page 110), and topping Rajma Nachos (page 174). Traditionally, the chutney calls for roasted, skinless peanuts, but I don't always have those in my pantry, so I started using peanut butter instead. Works just as well, if not better.

Combine all of the ingredients in a blender and blitz until smooth. If the consistency is too thick for your taste, thin it out with a teaspoon of water at a time.

Spicy Cilantro Chutney

6 to 8 green serrano peppers, cut in thirds

1 bunch cilantro (leaves and stems)

1 tablespoon cumin seeds

1 teaspoon salt

¾ cup water

3 tablespoons lemon juice

❄ FREEZER NOTE

This chutney is great to keep on hand in the freezer. I like to divide it up into a few portions and thaw the amount that I need in the fridge a day before I want to use it. The chutney will last for up to 5 days in an airtight container in the fridge.

This is not a subtle chutney and has some serious heat to it, but the kind of heat that still has flavor. I will never understand people who love to burn their taste buds off with heat so extreme it tastes like nothing but . . . heat? The cilantro and lemon juice add freshness. If you want a little less heat, carefully seed the serrano peppers (making sure to wash your hands thoroughly after) before adding them to the blender.

Put everything in a blender, with the serrano peppers at the bottom. Blend until the chutney is smooth.

Tamarind Chutney, 3 Ways

✳ **FREEZER NOTE**

If you're not planning on using the chutney on a regular basis, all three versions freeze well in an airtight container for many months. Just thaw in the fridge or on the counter before you use it.

There are several ways to make tamarind chutney, but you might be surprised to learn that two of those methods . . . don't involve any tamarind. Stay with me. The sweet-and-tangy chutney is traditionally made with tamarind, dates, jaggery or sugar, chili powder to balance out the sweetness, and a few spices (I keep mine simple with only cumin and Kashmiri red chili powder). Tamarind, however, wasn't always so readily available for Indian immigrants to the US, so they had to turn to other options. The first clever alternative is using amchur, or dried mango powder, as the tart element in the chutney. It's made in a similar fashion as the tamarind version, where the dates need to be softened and cooked down before being added to a blender. The other alternative requires zero cooking whatsoever. The secret ingredient? Apple butter. Some auntie figured out that apple butter was similar in texture and baseline flavor to tamarind chutney, especially if you blitz it with a few spices and a squeeze of lemon to give it that same tangy flavor. I did a taste test of all three versions side by side and while there are subtle differences, they all are delicious and, more importantly, all taste like tamarind chutney.

The chutney is extremely useful to keep on hand especially for when you want to make Tortilla Papdi Chaat (page 90), a quick Rice Krispie Bhel (page 77), Rajma Nachos (page 174), or a Tamarind Chutney Margarita (page 275). While you can use a store-bought version, they are often filled with preservatives and stabilizers, and can be too sweet. It's worth making your own.

1. WITH TAMARIND

1 cup pitted dates, preferably Medjool

¼ cup tamarind concentrate

1¼ cups water, divided

3 tablespoons sugar

½ teaspoon salt

1 teaspoon Kashmiri chili powder

1 teaspoon ground cumin

Combine the dates, tamarind, ½ cup water, sugar, and salt in an Instant Pot–safe or microwave-safe bowl. Cook for 3 minutes on high pressure in the Instant Pot, or cover and microwave for 3 minutes, stir and re-cover, and microwave for another 3 minutes. Transfer the date mixture to a blender, add the chili powder, cumin, and remaining ¾ cup water, and blend until smooth. Let the chutney cool before serving.

2. WITH AMCHUR

1 cup pitted dates, preferably Medjool

¼ cup amchur

1½ cups water, divided

3 tablespoons sugar

½ teaspoon salt

1 teaspoon Kashmiri chili powder

1 teaspoon ground cumin

Combine the dates, amchur, ½ cup water, sugar, and salt in an Instant Pot–safe or microwave-safe bowl. Cook for 3 minutes on high pressure in the Instant Pot, or cover and microwave for 3 minutes, stir and re-cover, and microwave for another 3 minutes. Transfer the date mixture to a blender, add the chili powder, cumin, and remaining 1 cup water, and blend until smooth. Let the chutney cool before serving.

3. WITH APPLE BUTTER

½ cup apple butter, preferably
    with no cinnamon

¾ cup water

1 tablespoon lemon juice

3 tablespoons sugar

1 teaspoon Kashmiri chili powder

1 teaspoon ground cumin

½ teaspoon salt

Combine all of the ingredients in a blender and blitz until well combined and smooth. Add more water if you prefer a thinner texture.

TAMARIND CHUTNEY

CILANTRO-MINT CHUTNEY

AMCHUR CHUTNEY

SPICY CILANTRO CHUTNEY

APPLE BUTTER CHUTNEY

Coconut Chutney

1 cup fresh or thawed frozen
   shredded coconut

¼ cup chana dal, roasted
   (sometimes called dalia)

1 green serrano pepper

1 teaspoon ginger paste *or* ¼-inch
   piece fresh ginger, grated

1 tablespoon plain full-fat yogurt

1 teaspoon salt

¾ cup water

TADKA

1 tablespoon neutral oil

½ teaspoon black mustard seeds

½ teaspoon cumin seeds

2 teaspoons urad dal

10 to 15 fresh curry leaves, torn in half

❄ FREEZER NOTE

You can freeze this chutney in an airtight container for up to 6 months. Thaw in the fridge overnight or at room temperature the day you want to use it. To make the chutney taste like you just made it, make the tadka fresh and pour it over the chutney just before serving.

Basic Plain Dosas (page 121) are incredibly delicious, but if we are being super honest here, half the reason anyone really eats them is because it's an excuse to eat a ridiculous amount of coconut chutney. The classic south Indian dish—I'm hesitant to call it a condiment because it is so much more than that—is incredibly versatile. It pairs well with the aforementioned dosas, Uttapam (page 129), idli (steamed fermented rice cakes), vada (fried lentil fritters), and so much more. I am willing to bet that the chutney also works with grilled fish or roasted vegetables that need some upgrading.

A good, strong blender is the key to this recipe. You can find shredded coconut in the frozen section at any Indian store. To make chutney with desiccated coconut, use hot water when you blend so that it helps rehydrate the coconut.

Put the coconut, chana dal, serrano pepper, ginger, yogurt, salt, and water in a blender and blend until smooth. You can add additional water to the blender if you prefer a thinner chutney, but I like how luxurious this tastes when it is on the thicker side, the consistency of good hummus. Spoon the chutney into a bowl.

Make the tadka, ideally immediately before serving. Heat the oil in a small saucepan over medium-high heat. Add the mustard seeds and, once they begin to pop, turn the heat down to low, add the cumin seeds and then the urad dal, and let the dal toast for 30 to 60 seconds. Remove the pan from the heat, add the curry leaves, and swirl the mixture. Pour the tadka over the chutney and serve.

Gunpowder Chutney

¼ cup white sesame seeds

2 tablespoons neutral oil

3½ ounces dried red chiles

30 to 40 fresh curry leaves

½ cup urad dal

¼ cup chana dal

3 tablespoons uncooked white rice

2 tablespoons whole black peppercorns

1½ teaspoons table salt

½ teaspoon hing (asafoetida)

 **INGREDIENT NOTE**

Hing, also known as asafoetida, is a powerful Indian spice that is often used to replace garlic. It's pretty pungent in nature, so a little bit goes a long way. It can easily be found at any Indian grocery store or online.

❄ FREEZER NOTE

When stored in an airtight container in a cool, dark place, gunpowder chutney can last for at least 6 months. When frozen, it can last for up to a year.

Gunpowder chutney is explosive in flavor, and rumor is that is how it got this very peculiar nickname. While it shows up as "gunpowder chutney" on most restaurant menus, it's better known as milagi podi, which translates to "chili powder." Podis are coarse spice mixes, or dry chutneys, commonly made with crushed lentils, dried chiles, curry leaves, and various other spices. South Indian cooking has hundreds of podis that vary from region to region and have different uses.

Historically, before refrigeration was commonplace, this podi was combined with ghee or oil and used to coat dosas and idli (steamed fermented rice cakes) to prevent them from becoming rock-hard when traveling long distances. It's still exceptional sprinkled, dry or combined with oil, on a Basic Plain Dosas (page 121), even if you aren't traveling. It's also very good stirred into yogurt as a dip of sorts, or tossed with a bowl of hot white rice for a quick meal. My preferred use? Mixing a spoonful into eggs before softly scrambling them.

As with most Indian spice blends, you can easily purchase this online or in an Indian grocery store, but it tastes fresher when made at home.

In a small heavy-bottomed saucepan, toast the sesame seeds over medium heat until they turn golden brown, about 1 minute. Pour the toasted sesame seeds into a small bowl and set aside. Add the oil to the same pan and let it get hot. Add the red chiles and sauté for 30 seconds. Add the curry leaves and cook until crispy, 1 to 2 minutes. Transfer the chiles and curry leaves to a plate or bowl and let them cool. Add a little more oil to the pan if needed and toast the urad and chana dal until golden brown, 3 to 4 minutes. Transfer the toasted dals to a blender, along with the sesame seeds, chiles, curry leaves, rice, peppercorns, salt, and hing. Blitz into a fine powder. Transfer to an airtight container and seal well.

Puli Inji

1 (2-inch) ball tamarind
  (not tamarind concentrate)

1 cup boiling water

2 tablespoons neutral oil, divided

1 cup finely chopped fresh ginger

1 green serrano pepper, finely minced

1 teaspoon Kashmiri red chili powder

½ teaspoon ground turmeric

½ cup jaggery

1½ teaspoons salt

½ teaspoon black mustard seeds

2 dried red chiles

15 fresh curry leaves

🥣 STORAGE NOTE

Puli inji will keep in an airtight container in the fridge for up to 3 months.

🍴 EXTRA CREDIT

I like to pile it on a wheel of Brie, then wrap the entire thing in puff pastry and bake it. Even easier: drizzle puli inji over a block of cream cheese and serve with crackers for a low-effort party appetizer.

Puli inji, frequently styled as inji puli, is a sweet-and-sour pickle from the southern Indian state of Kerala. Tamarind (puli) and ginger (inji) are cooked down together with a generous amount of jaggery, chiles, and spices like mustard seeds. The result is an Indian pickle that is wonderfully jammy in texture and tangy in flavor.

The pickle is a staple at Onam Sadhya, the multicourse meal served in celebration of Onam, or the harvest festival. Year-round, it's delicious paired with a bowl of rice and Sambar (page 131), served on the side of a Basic Plain Dosas (page 121), or spread on good bread to make a Puli Inji Grilled Cheese (page 109).

Put the tamarind in a bowl, cover it with the boiling water, and let soak for at least 10 minutes, until softened. Mash the tamarind between your fingers until it feels soft. Strain the tamarind water into a new bowl and squeeze as much liquid out of the tamarind pulp as possible. Set the tamarind water aside and discard the pulp.

Heat 1 tablespoon oil in a medium, heavy-bottomed saucepan over medium-high heat. Add the ginger and sauté for 5 to 6 minutes, until it starts to soften. Add the serrano pepper and cook for 1 minute, stirring occasionally. Add the tamarind water, chili powder, and turmeric and bring to a boil. Turn the heat down to low and let the mixture simmer for 15 minutes or so, until it starts to thicken. Add the jaggery and salt and stir to combine. Simmer for at least 2 minutes, until the jaggery is melted down and no clumps remain. Remove the pan from the heat.

To make the tadka, heat the remaining 1 tablespoon oil in a small saucepan over high heat. Add the mustard seeds and allow them to pop. Once they have stopped popping, add the dried chiles and curry leaves and turn off the heat. Sauté the mixture briefly, then add the tadka to the ginger-tamarind mixture. Give it a good mix to combine. Let the puli inji cool completely before serving

GARAM MASALA INGREDIENTS
(PAGE 62)

FENNEL SEEDS

CINNAMON STICKS

CARDAMOM SEEDS

CORIANDER
SEEDS

CLOVES

STAR ANISE

CUMIN SEEDS

GROUND NUTMEG

CHAAT MASALA INGREDIENTS
(PAGE 63)

SALT

CUMIN SEEDS

KALA NAMAK

KASHMIRI RED
CHILE POWDER

AMCHUR

BLACK PEPPERCORNS

Garam Masala

½ cup coriander seeds

¼ cup cumin seeds

3 tablespoons cardamom seeds

16 whole cloves

4 to 6 inches cinnamon sticks

4 star anise pods

2 teaspoons fennel seeds

1 teaspoon ground nutmeg

🥣 STORAGE NOTE

When stored in an airtight container in a cool, dark place, garam masala can last for at least 6 months, if not longer. Do not freeze the spice mix, as sometimes the flavor can change.

Garam masala might translate to "hot spices," but don't make the mistake of thinking that it is something that is light-your-mouth-on-fire spicy. "Garam" in this case points to the fact that it's a blend of warm spices that add a cozy layer of flavor to any dish. Every family has their own combination of spices that make their garam masala—maybe it's heavier on cumin, contains less cardamom, or has no star anise whatsoever. This is the blend my mom, Hina, likes to make, and the one I cooked with while growing up. Everything feels so rushed these days, but gently toasting your own spices, coaxing out their fragrances, is such a calming act. It requires you to slow down and really pay attention—even if only for a few minutes. A batch will last for at least six months stored in an airtight jar. (It makes a great gift!)

In a small saucepan, combine the coriander, cumin, cardamom seeds, cloves, cinnamon sticks, star anise, and fennel seeds. Toast the spices over medium-low heat, stirring constantly, until fragrant and toasty, 5 to 7 minutes. Remove the pan from the heat and carefully pour the spices onto a plate or wide bowl to let them cool. Add the nutmeg to the spices. When the spices are at room temperature, transfer to a spice grinder or blender and whizz into a fine powder. Transfer to an airtight container and seal well.

Chaat Masala

½ cup cumin seeds

½ cup amchur

¼ cup kala namak (black salt)

¼ cup Kashmiri red chili powder

¼ cup table salt

¼ cup ground black pepper

❦ INGREDIENT NOTE

You could purchase a chaat masala blend in stores. I like the mix from MDH or Everest. Making your own blend doesn't take dramatically more effort though.

◡ STORAGE NOTE

When stored in an airtight container in a cool, dark place, chaat masala can last for at least 6 months, if not longer. Do not freeze the spice mix, as sometimes the flavor can change.

You know that person you always invite to a party simply because they make any room they are in fun? This is the spice blend version of that friend. "Chaat" means "to lick," and chaat masala is a great way to add zip and zing to a dish. It's the ingredient that makes you smack your lips together trying to figure out what gives the dish its flavor. It's key to so many recipes throughout this book, including Masala Deviled Eggs (page 73), Masala Roasted Garlic Bread (page 261), and Pani Puri Mojito (page 273). It's even delicious just sprinkled over a bowl of freshly cut fruit, or stirred into some yogurt for a quick raita.

Chaat masala gets its distinct flavor from kala namak (black salt), which has a slightly sulfuric funk that makes things delicious, but you can't quite tell how or why. It also has some amchur (dried mango powder) to bring a nice pucker, and Kashmiri red chili powder for the gentle heat.

In a small saucepan, toast the cumin seeds over low heat while stirring constantly. Keep moving the cumin seeds around until they start to darken and smell super nutty, about 1 minute. Transfer to a spice grinder or mortar and pestle and crush the seeds into a powder.

In a jar, combine the cumin powder with the amchur, kala namak, chili powder, salt, and black pepper. Stir until well combined. Transfer to an airtight container and seal well.

Cucumber Raita

1 (1-pound) English cucumber, grated

3 cups full-fat yogurt
  (see Ingredient Note)

1 green serrano pepper,
  seeded and minced

½-inch piece fresh ginger, grated

1 tablespoon chopped fresh mint leaves

2 teaspoons Chaat Masala (page 63)

1 teaspoon salt

2 teaspoons neutral oil or ghee

1½ teaspoons cumin seeds

15 to 20 fresh curry leaves (optional)

🌿 INGREDIENT NOTE

You can use Greek yogurt in this recipe, but you will need to thin it out with at least ¼ cup water to achieve the right consistency.

🥣 STORAGE NOTE

Raita does not freeze well, but you can store it in an airtight container in the refrigerator for up to 4 days.

There are staple dishes in Indian cooking, building-block recipes that transcend singular regions, and raita is one of them. I don't know who first discovered that cucumber and yogurt make an excellent team, but you can look beyond India, too: Greek tzatziki, Turkish cacik, Lebanese khyar bi laban, and so on. What sets the Indian version apart is the tadka, or tempered spices, that are poured on top of the yogurt and stirred in at the end. This tadka is a simple one and calls for only two ingredients, cumin seeds and curry leaves. And while the curry leaves are technically optional, they take the raita to the next level and impart a fragrant, nutty aroma.

There's a tendency to want to explain Indian dishes in Western terms that aren't completely accurate. While raita can be both a dip and a sauce, that is not its true purpose on an Indian table. Raita serves as a cooling element, a wonderful foil to any hot or spicy elements. It's a dish that rounds out most meals. Make a batch to go with Rajma (page 191), Chana Masala (page 197), and especially the Biryani Baked in a Squash (page 159).

Squeeze the water out of the grated cucumber and set aside.

In a medium bowl, whisk the yogurt until super smooth. Mix in the cucumber, serrano pepper, ginger, mint, chaat masala, and salt and stir until well combined.

To make the tadka, heat the oil in a small saucepan over medium heat. Add the cumin seeds and let sizzle for 5 seconds. Turn off the heat and add the curry leaves, if using. Give the mixture a couple of swirls and then pour over the yogurt. Stir to combine well.

**MASALA CHAI INGREDIENTS
(PAGE 71)**

OBJECTS OF

The first person to spot five objects in a row wins the game and your

B | Taco Bell sauce packets stuffed into random kitchen drawers | Danish cookie tin not filled with cookies

I | Pond's Cold Cream | Second fridge filled with Indian food

N | Yogurt container not filled with yogurt | Johnnie Walker bottles

G | That straw broom | Kambal/winter blankets

O | 20-pound bags of basmati rice and atta | Vicks VapoRub

THE DIASPORA

Old-school family portrait with no one smiling	Plastic bags stuffed within plastic bags	Corelle plates
Coconut oil for cooking/hair	Bowls of cut fruit (it's a love language)	Plastic covers on remote controls
★	Trays of Ferrero Rocher (for guests)	Bags of safety pins for saris and clothes
Masala Dabba 	Shoe pile by the door	Nighties
Stainless steel plates, bowls, cups	Pressure cooker	Mini temple/deities in closets

SNACKS

Indians don't mess around when it comes to snacks. Come over to my home and I will offer you, at minimum, three to five snack options before you leave. On road trips, there may or may not be a suitcase filled with clothes, but there will definitely be a suitcase filled with snacks. More often than not, snack time and chai time are the same time, and because the chai tends to be sweet, the snacks are usually salty. In fact, in Gujarati, there is a special word for this category of food: farsan. They are so much more than fistfuls of popcorn or a pile of crackers: Indian snacks are a celebration of texture and flavor. But more importantly they are a celebration of time—none of them are meant to be eaten in a rush. It's a daily reminder to pause life for a few minutes to enjoy your favorites with a cup of chai—and ideally, the people you value the most.

& CHAI

Dad's Adu Ka Jaddu Masala Chai

½ cup water

½-inch piece fresh ginger, grated

4 green cardamom pods, smashed

4 to 5 fresh mint leaves

1 tablespoon loose black tea, such as Assam tea

½ cup 2% milk

1 tablespoon sugar

When I was eight years old, I asked my dad to cut me an apple as a snack. He obliged, and 10 minutes later, handed me a bowl containing what could generously be described as Picasso's next masterpiece—crafted out of a Gala apple. It was one of the few times I had seen him spend time in the kitchen, and I am not sure he has ever tried to cut another piece of fruit since, though that is probably for the best. (Love you, Dad!)

While his knife and cooking skills are terrible, my dad is a man of many talents. He is a deeply compassionate doctor, a truly wonderful singer, a master of poetry in several languages, and one of the friendliest people you will ever meet. My dad is also a man of many passions: he loves cars, maintaining his (still) thick head of hair, a great deal at Costco— and a proper cup of masala chai.

For him, masala chai is life. No matter what time of day it is, my dad will always say yes to a cup. Chai time is the one time when you will find him in the kitchen, lovingly watching over the pot of water as he tenderly adds in tea and spices. Though masala chai can be made with a cacophony of ingredients, like star anise and black pepper, my dad keeps it simple. He insists that the best cup is made with green cardamom pods, fresh mint leaves, and, most importantly, a hefty amount of fresh ginger. To the point that he has nicknamed his chai "adu ka jaddu," a dad joke in Gujarati that translates to "the magic of ginger."

Feel free to customize this to your own preferences (less sugar, nondairy milk), but do not skip the boiling process. This is what makes chai *chai*.

Recipe continues

Breakfast Cereal Chevvdo

4 cups puffed rice cereal

2 cups cornflakes

2 cups Rice Chex

2 cups Froot Loops

2 cups Kix

½ cup neutral oil

½ cup Spanish peanuts

½ cup cashew pieces

¼ cup dried curry leaves (optional)

2 teaspoons white sesame seeds

1 tablespoon salt

1 teaspoon ground turmeric

1 teaspoon Kashmiri red chili powder

1 cup black raisins

½ cup sugar

STORAGE NOTE

You can freeze chevvdo, but it's unnecessary to do so because it stays incredibly well in an airtight container at room temperature for up to 2 weeks.

I am not sure there is a recipe that is more representative of the way Indian food has evolved in America than breakfast cereal chevvdo. Chevvdo is an umbrella term for a type of Indian snack mix that is crunchy, spicy, salty, and often a little sweet at the same time. Unable to easily source ingredients like fried lentils and flattened rice, common ingredients in many chevvdo styles, enterprising immigrant cooks turned to American breakfast cereals, which were affordable but offered the same crispy textures.

It's very common to make this snack mix with only cornflakes, but my mom and aunties would throw in whatever cereal they had on hand. The mix below is my preferred combination of cereals—I like the sweetness and color that Froot Loops add—but feel free to customize the cereal selection with whatever you might want to use up. A small bowl of chevvdo pairs well with a glass of milk or a cup of masala chai, but it's also a convenient portable snack—I love it on a road trip.

Combine the cereals in a large bowl and mix well.

Heat the oil in a large, heavy-bottomed pot over medium heat. Add the peanuts and cook, stirring constantly, until they are gently browned, 2 to 3 minutes. Turn the heat down to medium-low, add the cashews, and stir for about 1 minute, until they are toasted. Add the curry leaves (if using) and sesame seeds and stir until well combined. Turn the heat down to a simmer and add the salt, turmeric, and chili powder. Pour in the cereal mix, turn the heat up to medium, and let the cereal toast for 5 minutes, stirring every 30 seconds. The cereal should smell quite nutty at this point. Turn off the heat. Add the raisins, then sprinkle the sugar over the raisins and cereal. Stir until the mix is well combined, then quickly transfer the snack mix to an airtight storage container so the sugar doesn't burn. Let cool before sealing.

Rice Krispie Bhel

3 cups puffed rice cereal

1 Roma tomato, diced

¼ red onion, diced

1 medium red potato, boiled, peeled, and diced

¼ cup Spicy Green Chutney (page 51)

¾ cup Tamarind Chutney (page 52)

Pinch salt

Generous handful fresh cilantro

½ cup sev (optional, see Ingredient Note)

¼ cup pomegranate arils (optional)

❧ INGREDIENT NOTE

Sev are small, thin fried noodles made of chickpea flour. You can find them in any Indian grocery store, and you can store them in an airtight container in the fridge for at least a year so they won't get stale.

❄ FREEZER NOTE

Bhel does not freeze, or keep in the fridge. I can't emphasize this enough: please consume immediately.

Whenever my mom whips out her giant stainless steel mixing bowl, my mouth automatically starts to water, in a very Pavlovian response. I know if that bowl is out, she is very likely about to make a batch of bhel—one of my all-time favorite Indian street foods. The base is made from roasted mumra, or puffed rice, plus sev (see Ingredient Note), and papdi (essentially a deep-fried cracker). That mix gets tossed with a host of fresh ingredients, like diced tomato, cilantro, onion, and plenty of chutney. It's one of those snacks that hits almost every note: salty, spicy, sour, tangy, herbaceous, and sweet all in one.

While bhel is easy to put together once you have the ingredients, not everyone always has mumra around, so my mom cleverly started substituting puffed rice cereal whenever the craving would hit. Bhel made with mumra becomes soggy fast, but bhel made with puffed rice cereal becomes soggy even faster, so it can be a race to the finish line once the chutneys are added to the bowl. Any leftover cereal can be used in the Breakfast Cereal Chevvdo (page 74) or in a tray of Jaggery and Fennel Rice Krispie Treats (page 302).

In a large bowl, combine the cereal, tomato, onion, potato, green chutney, tamarind chutney, and salt. Give it a good toss until everything is evenly coated. Sprinkle on the cilantro, sev (if using), and pomegranate (if using), mix well, and serve immediately.

Masala Poutine

FRIES

1 (26-ounce) package frozen french fries

GRAVY

2 tablespoons neutral oil

2 tablespoons garlic paste *or*
  6 garlic cloves, minced

1 (6-ounce) can tomato paste

1 tablespoon Garam Masala (page 62)

1½ teaspoons salt

1 teaspoon Kashmiri red chili powder

1 teaspoon ground turmeric

1 teaspoon ground cumin

1 teaspoon ground coriander

2 cups water or broth

1 teaspoon sugar

¼ cup heavy cream

PANEER AND CURDS

2 teaspoons neutral oil

4 ounces paneer, cut into ½-inch cubes

5 to 6 ounces cheese curds or low-moisture
  mozzarella cubes (see Ingredient Note)

Chopped scallions, for garnish

🌿 INGREDIENT NOTE

You want plain (not breaded) cheese curds for this recipe. You can find them in the cheese section of a number of grocery stores (I buy mine at Target). If you cannot find curds, cubes of mozzarella or chunks of halloumi would work, too.

You might be thinking, "A poutine recipe, Khushbu? Really? Isn't that Canadian? I thought your book was called *Amrikan*." And that is fair! But versions of poutine with desi ingredients have been popping up on the menus of every trendy Indian restaurant around the country for the past decade. From what I can tell, this is thanks to the Indian Canadian family behind the Los Angeles restaurant Badmaash. The Mahendros have had a chicken tikka poutine made with masala fries, beef gravy, and cheese curds on the menu since they first opened in 2013. I've seen endless variations on menus ever since: butter chicken poutine, chana masala poutine, keema poutine, saag poutine, and so on and so forth. The combination of fries + saucy element + cheese curds is always going to be delicious.

This recipe is my platonic ideal of an Indian poutine. I want a rich, deeply spiced gravy that tastes somewhere in between the base for Classic Butter Chicken (page 188) and the base for Paneer Tikka Masala (page 185). I love a good, squeaky, just-starting-to-melt cheese curd on my poutine, but also with grilled paneer pieces for a double cheese element. If you can't find paneer, halloumi would also taste excellent. As for the base, use whichever shape of fry you like the best. I recommend using a bag of frozen fries because making great fries from scratch is too much work. Don't skip the flourish of scallions at the end—the sharp notes of the allium are necessary for cutting through the richness of the gravy.

Prepare the fries according to the package instructions.

Meanwhile, to make the gravy, heat the oil in a medium saucepan over medium heat. Add the garlic and sauté for 1 minute, or until golden. Add the tomato paste and stir for 2 to 3 minutes, until the paste darkens in color. Reduce the heat to low and add the garam masala, salt, chili powder, turmeric, cumin, and coriander. Stir until everything is well combined and sauté for about 4 minutes to cook out the raw flavor of the tomato paste. Stir in the water and sugar, bring to a simmer, and cook for about 10 minutes, until the sauce thickens. Remove from the heat and stir in the cream. Set aside, covered to keep warm.

When the fries are done, fry the paneer. Heat the oil in a large skillet over medium heat. Add the cubes of paneer and fry until golden, about a minute on each side.

Spread out the fries on a large serving tray. Douse the fries with the tomato gravy. Scatter the curds and paneer over the saucy fries and allow the curds to gently melt. Garnish with scallions and serve immediately.

MASALA DEVILED
EGGS (PAGE 73)

MASALA POUTINE
(PAGE 78)

TANDOORI CHICKEN
WINGS (PAGE 86)

Kale Pakoras

1 bunch curly kale

2 cups besan flour

2 teaspoons ground cumin

1 teaspoon Garam Masala (page 62)

½ teaspoon ground turmeric

½ teaspoon Kashmiri red chili powder

½ teaspoon salt

1¼ cups water

Neutral oil, for frying

Cilantro-Mint Chutney
    (page 50), for serving

Tamarind Chutney (page 52),
    for serving

✳ FREEZER NOTE

You can freeze cooked pakoras in an air-tight container with a layer or parchment paper separating each one for up to a month. Reheat in an air fryer or oven.

I am convinced that Indians can transform nearly anything into a pakora. I can't promise that every ingredient *should* be turned into a pakora, but it absolutely *could* be turned into a pakora. Of the many deep-fried things around the globe, pakoras are one of my favorites because they feature a batter made of besan, or chickpea flour, plus a handful of spices and seasonings. The result is a golden coating that is denser and more savory than a tempura batter.

Ingredients that you will commonly find as a pakora: potato, eggplant, whole chiles, strips of paneer, and boneless chicken pieces, to name a few. Ingredients that you won't often find as a pakora: kale. However, I've started to notice a growing number of Indian restaurants around the US adding kale pakoras to their menu. (The best ones can be found at Adda in New York City.) Even though kale is not native to India and therefore not commonly found in Indian cooking, it works well as a pakora. The batter forms a crunchy crackly armor around each leaf, which is best dunked into both Cilantro-Mint Chutney (page 50) and Tamarind Chutney (page 52) just before eating.

Wash the kale and dry it thoroughly. Remove and discard the stems and tear the leaves in half horizontally. Set aside.

In a medium bowl, whisk together the besan flour, cumin, garam masala, turmeric, chili powder, and salt. Add the water and whisk again. The batter should have the consistency of thick pancake batter.

Heat at least 3 inches of oil in a wok or large, heavy-bottomed pot to 350 degrees F. Dip a kale leaf into the batter so that both sides are coated and shake off the excess, then add it to the oil. Repeat the process, frying 2 or 3 leaves at a time for 3 minutes or so, until crisp on both sides. Drain on a paper towel–lined plate. Continue until all the kale is used up. Serve with both chutneys for dipping.

Chili Cheese Toast

2 tablespoons cream cheese or whipped
   cream cheese, at room temperature

4 slices white sandwich bread

½ cup shredded cheese (mozzarella
   + cheddar is ideal)

2 tablespoons finely chopped red onion

2 tablespoons finely chopped
   red bell pepper

2 tablespoons finely chopped
   green bell pepper

6 to 8 pickled jalapeños, finely chopped

2 tablespoons minced fresh cilantro

1 tablespoon Chaat Masala (page 63)

½ teaspoon garlic powder

¼ teaspoon dried oregano
   or Italian seasoning

Ketchup, for serving

❋ INGREDIENT NOTE

As for the cheese, I prefer a blend of mozzarella and cheddar, but use any cheese that you like, as long as it melts well. Make sure to shred the cheese yourself. Pre-shredded cheeses are often coated so they do not clump, but this coating can sometimes prevent it from melting.

❋ FREEZER NOTE

This does not freeze well.

I will never understand how avocado became the most famous of the toasts, when chili cheese toast exists. This isn't to say that avocado toast isn't delicious, but the combination of cheese, green chiles, and chaat masala is unrivaled—I want to eat it for breakfast, lunch, and dinner.

Many versions (including this one) feature tiny pieces of bell pepper folded into the melty cheese, which gives the dish a nice texture. (You can leave these out if you hate bell peppers!) I like to slather my bread with cream cheese before adding the other toppings because of the creaminess it brings to the toast. I also use pickled jalapeños because they're milder, and that pickled flavor complements everything here so well.

Preheat the oven to 375 degrees F. Line a rimmed baking sheet with parchment paper.

Spread ½ tablespoon cream cheese evenly across each slice of bread and place on the prepared baking sheet.

In a small bowl, combine the shredded cheese, onion, bell peppers, jalapeños, and cilantro and mix well. Stir in the chaat masala, garlic powder, and oregano. Divide the cheese mixture evenly between the slices of bread, spreading it evenly across the cream cheese mixture.

Bake the toasts for 7 to 9 minutes, until the cheese is melty and the bread is crispy. Cut each toast into 3 strips or 4 triangles. Serve with ketchup for dipping.

Tandoori Chicken Wings

¾ cup full-fat Greek yogurt

2 tablespoons lemon juice

1 tablespoon garlic paste
  or 3 garlic cloves, minced

1 tablespoon ginger paste or 1-inch
  piece fresh ginger, grated

1 tablespoon Kashmiri red chili powder

1 tablespoon kasoori methi (optional,
  but really makes the dish)

2 teaspoons salt

1½ teaspoons Garam Masala (page 62)

½ teaspoon ground coriander

½ teaspoon ground turmeric

2 pounds chicken wings (see
  Ingredient Note)

Neutral oil, for greasing

❦ INGREDIENT NOTE

You can use whatever kind of wing you like, including boneless. I like to buy bone-in frozen wings that are already separated into flats and drums.

❄ FREEZER NOTE

You can freeze marinated uncooked chicken wings in an airtight container for up to 3 months. Let them thaw in the fridge and cook within 24 hours.

I am not sure there is a dish that is more Indian and American than a plate of tandoori chicken wings. It's essentially the technique behind tandoori chicken—cooking meat marinated in spiced yogurt—applied to the beloved chicken wing. The yogurt marinade is the easiest way to ensure the wings remain juicy while also being flavor-packed. Tandoori chicken is typically cooked in a clay oven (tandoor), something most people do not have at home. These wings are baked in a regular oven but then broiled at the end to give the meat the wonderful char it would receive in a tandoor. These are easy to whip up for a party, or when you're bored of your typical game day snacks. And if you don't want to use meat, this works well with cauliflower florets instead of chicken. I like to serve the wings (chicken or cauliflower) with a dip, where I fold a few spoonfuls of Spicy Cilantro Chutney (page 51) into sour cream or plain Greek yogurt. They are also great dunked in the Amchur Ranch from the salad on page 237.

In a medium bowl, combine the yogurt, lemon juice, garlic, ginger, chili powder, kasoori methi (if using), salt, garam masala, coriander, and turmeric. Mix to combine well. Add the wings to the bowl and toss, making sure each piece of chicken is fully coated in the marinade. Cover and let the chicken marinate in the fridge for at least 1 hour.

Preheat the oven to 400 degrees F. Line a rimmed baking sheet with aluminum foil and place a wire rack on top, then grease the rack with a little oil.

Place the wings on the prepared rack and bake for 35 to 40 minutes, until the chicken is cooked through. Move the baking sheet up to the top rack, turn the oven to broil, and broil the wings for 2 to 3 minutes so that the skin gets crisp and a little charred.

Peanut Chaat

½ cup diced red bell pepper

½ cup diced cucumber

½ cup diced white onion

½ cup minced fresh cilantro

1 cup salted roasted peanuts

1½ cups pomegranate arils (optional)

Juice of 1 lemon

2 teaspoons Chaat Masala (see page 63)

1 teaspoon Kashmiri red chili powder

1 teaspoon salt

❄ **FREEZER NOTE**

This does not freeze well.

If you like foods with a ton of snap and crunch, this is *the* chaat for you. It's the dish my mom often makes me when I tear into the kitchen hangry, in need of a snack that has some actual substance but isn't too heavy. There are no fried elements to this chaat, or any chutneys you need to premake. Dice whatever crunchy fresh vegetables you have on hand, toss it with some peanuts, lemon juice, and chaat masala, and you're ready to go. It's a quick appetizer for a dinner party, and adaptable to what you have on hand. Try adding diced radish, carrot, or jicama to the chaat, or swapping out the pomegranate arils for diced apple. This chaat is essentially a salad disguised as a snack.

In a medium bowl, combine the bell pepper, cucumber, onion, cilantro, peanuts, and pomegranate arils (if using). Add the lemon juice, chaat masala, chili powder, and salt and toss until evenly combined. Divide into 4 bowls and enjoy right away.

Harsha Auntie's Khichu

8 cups water

1 tablespoon white sesame seeds

1½ teaspoons cumin seeds

3 or 4 whole cloves

½ cinnamon stick

4 cups rice flour

1 tablespoon salt, plus more for serving

3 green serrano peppers, diced

1 teaspoon baking soda

Neutral oil, for serving

Kashmiri red chili powder, for serving

◉ SERVING NOTE

Like Harsha Auntie, I like to roll the khichu into small spheres before steaming them, but you can shape it however you like—I've seen people make them into little doughnuts or logs, or steam them in small bowls and flip them out before serving them with a dip of oil mixed with salt and Kashmiri red chili powder.

❈ FREEZER NOTE

Khichu can be frozen in an airtight container for up to 1 month. To reheat, thaw in the fridge first, then heat in the microwave or steam again until warm.

Between kindergarten and ninth grade, I lived next door to Harsha Auntie and her family. Since they were such close family friends of ours, it was super convenient for my mom— she could easily borrow ingredients and split carpooling—and it was great for me because I had unlimited access to their giant trampoline. I especially loved to visit whenever Harsha Auntie would make her famous khichu. It's one of my favorite dishes, and I have yet to eat a version better than hers.

Khichu, which is also known as papdi nu lot, is a very Gujarati dish. It's made with rice flour that is twice cooked. The consistency is between a thick polenta and a loose mochi. It technically is a snack meant to be served with chai, but in my household, if it was Harsha Auntie's khichu, it quickly became a meal. I spent an afternoon in her kitchen with a pen and notebook, forcing her to stop and measure ingredients as she went along so that I could learn to perfectly recreate it.

In a large pot, combine the water, sesame seeds, cumin seeds, cloves, and cinnamon stick. Bring to a boil.

Meanwhile, in a medium bowl, whisk together the rice flour and salt.

When the water is boiling, stir in the serrano peppers and baking soda. Slowly add the flour mixture and turn the heat down to low, stirring constantly until the mixture is evenly combined. It will be super thick. Remove the pot from the heat and let the batter cool down for 10 minutes.

Pour an inch or two of water into another large pot and add a steamer basket. Bring the water to a boil. Dip your hands in cold water to prevent the dough from sticking to them, and shape the dough into 2- to 3-inch balls. Place the balls in the steamer, cover, and let them cook for 15 minutes. Serve the khichu with oil, salt, and chili powder for dipping.

Tortilla Papdi Chaat

Neutral oil, for frying

2 (10-inch) flour tortillas

¼ cup plain yogurt, preferably full-fat

2 tablespoons water

1 teaspoon Chaat Masala
(page 63), divided

Pinch salt

½ (15-ounce) can chickpeas,
drained and rinsed

1 medium red potato, boiled,
peeled, and diced

¼ cup Tamarind Chutney (page 52)

2 tablespoons Spicy Cilantro
Chutney (page 51)

¼ cup diced red onion

¼ cup nylon sev (optional but highly
recommended; see Ingredient Note)

Generous handful chopped fresh cilantro

🌿 INGREDIENT NOTE

You can find nylon sev (very thin sev) at
most Indian grocery stores. Leftovers will
keep in your fridge or freezer for several
months.

❄ FREEZER NOTE

Do not freeze this. Consume the dish
immediately.

Papdi chaat is the ideal snack when you need to feed a small
crowd and want something fun but not fussy. It consists of
papdi, a deep-fried cracker of sorts, loaded up with toppings
like boiled potatoes and chickpeas, then drizzled with
multiple chutneys. It is everything I love in a savory snack:
crunchy, but with soft elements, lots of sauce, and plenty
of raw onion. I have yet to meet someone who doesn't like
papdi chaat.

I am thankful that resourceful immigrant aunties didn't
let limited access to papdi get in the way of making this
dish. Instead, they started deep-frying strips of flour tortillas, which were more readily available. The substitute works
incredibly well or, in my opinion, even better. The only way
to take it to the next level? Top the papdi chaat with a fistful
of pomegranate.

Pour ½ inch of oil into a Dutch oven or large, deep skillet and
heat over medium-high heat. Cut the tortillas into diamonds
or squares that are about ½ inch wide. Working in batches as
necessary, fry the tortilla pieces until they are golden brown,
then transfer to a paper towel–lined plate to drain. These are
your "papdi."

In a small bowl, whisk together the yogurt and water until it's
thin enough to drizzle. Mix in ½ teaspoon chaat masala and
the salt.

Once the papdi have cooled, arrange them in a single layer on
a large plate. Scatter the chickpeas and potato evenly over the
papdi. Sprinkle the remaining ½ teaspoon chaat masala over
the chickpeas and potatoes. Drizzle the seasoned yogurt over
the chickpeas and potato, then repeat with the tamarind and
cilantro chutneys. Scatter the onion, sev (if using, but it's truly so
much better with it), and cilantro on top and serve immediately!
This gets soggy fast.

Q & A ON EATING MI

Why does this Q&A even exist?
The Indian American diaspora has a very complicated relationship with meat! (And I think it's worth
explaining.)

*Okay, fine. I thought most Indians were vegetar-
ian anyways?*
It might feel that way because those who are
vegetarians tend to be staunch vegetarians. But
this is a common misconception. It's estimated that
only 23 to 40 percent of Indians in India follow a
meat-free diet. I was unable to find any hard data
on what percentage of Indians in the American
diaspora follow a strictly vegetarian diet, but many
will eat everything from butter chicken to burgers.

*If most Indians eat meat, does that mean the
majority of recipes in this book contain meat?*
Not quite. I wanted this cookbook to be an accurate
reflection of how members of this diaspora cook
and eat. So, while some recipes include meat, most
are vegetarian or are easily made vegetarian. Even
if someone in the diaspora eats meat, many of the

other dishes they consume regularly are vegetarian. The idea of a "meat and potatoes" diet doesn't
really exist in Indian culture.

*But I noticed there is not a single cow in the
book. What's your beef with beef?*
This isn't about believing that cows are sacred
(as some Hindus believe). Plenty of Indians eat
beef. I simply don't love huge hunks of the protein.
I developed these recipes to work without beef,
but you could easily use it when making recipes
like Mushroom Pepper Fry (page 229) or Mushroom
Keema Pasta (page 161).

*I also noticed there is no lamb or pork (except
some optional bacon) in the book. Why?*
Lamb, mutton, and goat are common animal proteins
consumed in Indian cooking, along with pork (unless
you are Muslim), but I chose to not use them to show
that red meat is not necessary for any of the recipes.
Also, as someone who does worry about the planet,
I wanted to focus more on what vegetables can do,
and how easy they can be to cook.

So you're saying that the majority of Indians eat meat, though depending on who they are, they only eat some types of meat, except for the ones that absolutely do not? This is confusing. Help!

Indians historically have a complicated and complex relationship with meat. That relationship can be dependent upon many factors—religion, caste, wealth, and gender, to name a few. A lot of these beliefs have translated over to the diaspora, especially since many diasporic Indians hail from upper caste cultures (more on that on page 198), which tend to be vegetarian.

Gender? Really?

I've seen entire families be vegetarian, or often just the women (wives, daughters) in a family remain vegetarian while the men eat meat. There are others (of any gender) who are from vegetarian families but started to eat meat out of a desire to fit into American culture.

What about the kids born in America?

There are those born into vegetarian households in the diaspora who eat meat outside of the house when their parents aren't around. There are also those kids born into meat-eating households that eat "forbidden" proteins when out with their friends. Eating beef or pork is a classic form of South Asian teenage rebellion. There are also plenty of Indian Americans who float somewhere in between, eating only chicken or only chicken and turkey, and perhaps a bit of seafood (or only seafood!). They tend to avoid a lot of red meat like beef and pork—for reasons that are religious, but also not.

What's your personal philosophy around cooking and eating meat?

Do what makes you happy. I grew up in a vegetarian family, and that is where I try to remain for a few reasons that include cost, ease, and the planet.

The planet?

Yeah! The Earth rules. Global warming does not.

If (and that is a big IF) there was one upside to the British colonization of India, it was the introduction of tea sandwiches to the subcontinent. But of course, Indians managed to improve upon the dainty sandwiches by adding several layers of flavor. (A generous swipe of green chutney or sprinkle of chaat masala is what they were always missing.) And it doesn't stop there. If there is a sandwich format, Indian flavors will always take it to the next level. Just ask the veggie burger, or the grilled cheese, or the club sandwich . . .

SANDV

ICHES

Chutney Tea Sandwiches

2 teaspoons full-fat cream cheese
or whipped cream cheese, at
room temperature (optional
but highly recommended)

4 slices white sandwich
bread, crusts cut off

4 teaspoons Cilantro-Mint
Chutney (page 50)

2 slices gouda, provolone, or
another soft white cheese

1 Roma tomato, thinly sliced

½ Persian cucumber, thinly sliced

1 teaspoon Chaat Masala (page 63)

❄ FREEZER NOTE
I wouldn't freeze these! Best consumed
fresh.

These sandwiches, an improvement upon the British classic, are best made with a thin, squishy white bread. They were one of my favorite snacks my mom would pack for us on road trips as they hold up extremely well at room temperature. As an adult, I often make a riff on this sandwich (with heartier bread) on the days I'm craving a lighter lunch. I spread chutney on both slices of bread, but you may prefer to spread one slice with butter or jam/marmalade, and chutney on the other. Just make sure to always cut off the crusts—that makes it a true tea sandwich.

I like the tangy note cream cheese brings to the sandwiches. If you hate tomatoes, feel free to leave them out, but do not skip the cucumber! It gives the sandwiches their signature crunch. And, yes, they go well with a cup of masala chai or any tea of your choice.

Spread 1 teaspoon cream cheese (if using) on 2 slices of bread, spread 1 teaspoon chutney over the cream cheese, and then spread 1 teaspoon chutney on the remaining 2 slices. If not using cream cheese, just spread 1 teaspoon chutney on each slice. On 2 of the slices, place a slice of cheese, then layer on half of the tomato slices and half of the cucumber slices in 2 even, flat layers. Sprinkle ½ teaspoon chaat masala over the vegetables. Cover with the remaining 2 slices of bread, chutney side down. Cut both sandwiches in halves or thirds and serve.

Masala Veggie Burgers

3 small red potatoes, boiled and peeled

1 medium sweet potato, boiled and peeled

1 (15-ounce) can black beans, drained and rinsed

2 carrots, peeled and grated

¾ cup frozen corn kernels

¾ cup frozen green peas

3 tablespoons oats (not steel-cut)

1 tablespoon garlic paste
   or 3 garlic cloves, minced

1 tablespoon Garam Masala (page 62)

2 teaspoons Kashmiri red chili powder

2 teaspoons sugar

1½ teaspoons salt

Neutral oil, for cooking

Sliced cheddar cheese or cheese of your choice (optional)

FOR ASSEMBLY

Butter, for griddling

5 or 6 burger buns

¼ cup Tamarind Chutney (page 52)

¼ cup ketchup

Lettuce

Tomato slices

Red or white onion slices

❄ **FREEZER NOTE**

To freeze the uncooked patties, place them on a rimmed baking sheet lined with parchment paper. Once the patties are frozen, transfer them to an airtight container or ziplock bag and store in the freezer for up to 3 months. The cooked veggie burgers also freeze well.

This veggie burger is the love child of vada pav, which is basically a deep-fried orb of spiced potatoes between bread, and a veggie burger that has actual vegetables in it (none of this faux tech meat stuff).

I keep the toppings simple—too many toppings make the burgers too tall to eat, and I am uninterested in participating in the unhinged jaw Olympics. And for the optimal eating experience, I also like to make the patties slightly smaller than the size of whichever burger buns I am using.

In a medium bowl, mash the red potatoes, sweet potato, and black beans until mostly smooth. The mixture should be easy to mold into patties with your hands. Fold in the carrots, corn, peas, oats, garlic garam masala, chili powder, sugar, and salt and mix until well combined. With your hands, form the mixture into 10 or 12 patties that are 3 to 4 inches in diameter, depending on the size of bun. If the mixture feels a little too wet or is struggling to bind together, add more oats.

Heat a bit of oil in a large nonstick skillet or griddle over medium-high heat. Place 2 to 4 patties in the pan. Cook until browned on the bottom, about 3 minutes, then flip and cook on the other side for another 3 minutes or so. The outside of the burgers should be somewhat crispy while the interior remains soft. Transfer to a plate and repeat until all the burgers are cooked. If you want melty cheese on your burgers, add a slice on top of each patty, add a splash of water to the pan, and cover for about 30 seconds.

Wipe out the pan before using it to griddle the buns. Butter the burger buns generously and cook, buttered sides down, over medium heat until crispy.

In a small bowl, mix together the tamarind chutney and ketchup. Spread the mixture across the griddled sides of each bun. Place a patty on each bottom bun, top with lettuce, tomato, and onion, and then the top buns.

Hash Brown, Egg, and Cheese Kati Rolls

4 Super Flaky Parathas (page 247) or store-bought frozen parathas (see Ingredient Note on page 29)

4 large eggs

2 tablespoons milk

Olive oil or neutral oil, for frying

Salt and ground black pepper to taste

4 thin slices cheddar or American cheese

2 frozen hash brown patties, prepared according to package instructions

2 tablespoons Spicy Cilantro Chutney (page 51)

¼ red onion, thinly sliced

4 strips bacon, cooked (optional)

Ketchup, for serving (optional)

⊚ SERVING NOTE

You could easily add a strip or two of bacon if that is what you crave, or even a slice of ripe avocado. If you don't want to make green chutney, a good hot sauce would work instead.

I used to eat kati rolls from the Kati Roll Company at least twice a week while working at my egregiously underpaid, first full-time food writing job at a miserable midtown NYC office building. It was a terrible situation where I cried nearly every day, but a mere three blocks away was one of the few affordable lunch options where I could find solace. My go-to kati roll—which is somewhere in between a wrap and burrito—was always the unda roll, in which a layer of beaten egg is cooked onto a paratha, topped with chutney and raw onion, and rolled up.

Now that I no longer have to trek to midtown for that awful job, I make my kati rolls at home. One day I woke up craving a breakfast burrito but was out of tortillas, so I decided to make a kati roll that combined my favorite elements of both dishes: the thin layer of egg directly on the paratha of the kati roll, with the melty cheese and crunchy hash browns, cornerstones of a good breakfast burrito. It all gets drizzled with Spicy Cilantro Chutney (page 51) and topped with a pile of raw red onions.

Recipe continues

In a small bowl, whisk together the flour, milk, kasoori methi, chili powder, salt, and black pepper. It should be a little runnier than pancake batter. Put the bread crumbs in another small bowl to create a little breading station. One by one, dip each square of paneer into the flour-milk mixture to evenly cover the paneer. Then dredge the paneer in the bread crumbs and make sure the surface is well coated (you can press the bread crumbs on with your fingers). Place the coated paneer on a plate.

Heat 2 to 3 inches of oil to 300 degrees F in a large pot or deep cast-iron skillet. Working in batches as necessary, fry the paneer on both sides until golden brown, 2 to 3 minutes. Transfer to a paper towel–lined plate.

Heat another skillet or a griddle over medium heat. Spread a little butter on the cut sides of each bun and griddle them until they have lacy, crispy edges. Spread a thin layer of the tandoori mayonnaise on the griddled sides of each bun. Place a piece of paneer on each bottom bun. Top with a pile of shredded lettuce (All hail, shredduce!), then cover with the top buns.

Keralan Fried Chicken Sandwiches

1 cup buttermilk

2 tablespoons garlic paste *or* 6 garlic cloves, minced

1 tablespoon ginger paste *or* 1-inch piece fresh ginger, grated

3 green serrano peppers, seeded if desired

½ bunch fresh cilantro

½ bunch fresh mint

1½ teaspoons salt

1 teaspoon Garam Masala (page 62)

4 boneless, skinless chicken thighs, trimmed

CURRY LEAF MAYO

2 tablespoons neutral oil

15 to 20 fresh curry leaves

2 tablespoons white sesame seeds

1 tablespoon garlic paste *or* 3 garlic cloves, minced

¼ cup mayonnaise

FOR FRYING AND ASSEMBLY

Neutral oil, for frying

1 cup all-purpose flour

1 teaspoon salt

10 to 20 fresh curry leaves, for garnish

Ghee or butter, for griddling

4 hamburger buns

12 bread and butter pickle chips

I've always wondered why KFC has never capitalized on the genius that is the other KFC, or Keralan Fried Chicken. (Sorry, the dad joke had to happen!) I have this theory that the way to make Indian food truly popular in the United States, in a big mass-market way, is through fried chicken. If the past decade has proven anything, it is that Americans are obsessed with deep-fried chicken, and with the fried chicken sandwich in particular. There are several types of Indian fried chicken styles, but this is my favorite. Kerala-style fried chicken has a pleasant mild heat; it won't blow your tongue off. And it's spiffed up with fresh herbs like cilantro and mint and crowned with crispy curry leaves.

This chicken recipe is inspired by Atlanta-based chef Asha Gomez, and the brilliant version in her cookbook *My Two Souths*. Traditionally, the chicken is marinated in coconut milk, but Gomez swaps that out for buttermilk, a staple in many Southern fried chicken recipes. I prefer the texture and flavor that buttermilk imparts.

I have never seen Keralan fried chicken served as a sandwich—but it's something I've always believed would be delicious. I created a simple curry leaf mayo to play up the flavors in the chicken. Definitely griddle your favorite buns in plenty of butter or ghee before constructing the sandwich, and don't forget the bread and butter pickles—they add a nice pop of salt. If you are vegetarian or don't want to eat fried chicken, this marinade works well with cauliflower, paneer, and oyster mushrooms, too. There is no reason KFC can't stand for Keralan Fried Cauliflower.

Recipe continues

❄ FREEZER NOTE

Fried chicken can be frozen in an airtight container for up to 3 months.

To make the marinade, combine the buttermilk, garlic, ginger, serrano peppers, cilantro, mint, salt, and garam masala in a blender and puree until smooth. (If not marinating the chicken the same day, cover and refrigerate the marinade for up to 2 days.)

Put 1 chicken thigh in a gallon-size freezer bag. Press the air out of the bag (but don't seal it), then pound the chicken using a rolling pin or a meat tenderizer until it's ¼ to ½ inch thick. (This depends on your preference: if you want a juicier sandwich, go for ½ inch thick.) Set the pounded thigh to the side, and repeat with the remaining 3 thighs. Put all 4 thighs in the bag and pour in the marinade. Seal and shake to make sure that each piece of chicken is well coated. Refrigerate for at least 12 hours or up to 24 hours.

On the day you want to eat the sandwiches, make the curry leaf mayo. In a small skillet, heat the oil over medium heat until it is shimmering. Add the curry leaves, sesame seeds, and garlic and give it a good stir. Turn off the heat and continue to let the curry leaves crisp. Let the mixture cool. Put the mayo in a small bowl, add the cooled curry leaf mixture, and give it a good stir. Wipe out the pan—you will use it to griddle the buns.

When you are ready to fry the chicken, pour a couple inches of neutral oil into a large, heavy-bottomed pot or deep skillet and heat until it hits 350 degrees F. Line a rimmed baking sheet with aluminum foil and place a wire rack on it.

In a shallow dish, whisk together the flour and salt. Shake off the excess marinade from the chicken thighs and dredge each one in the flour mixture, making sure it is evenly coated.

Working in batches as necessary, fry the chicken until golden brown and cooked through, 4 to 5 minutes per side. Let the chicken cool on the prepared rack.

While the chicken is cooling, quickly fry the curry leaves in the hot oil until they are crisp, about 10 seconds. Sprinkle the curry leaves on the chicken.

Reheat the small skillet over medium heat. Spread ghee on the cut sides of each bun and griddle until crisp and golden. Spread a light layer of curry leaf mayo on the griddled sides of each bun. Place a fried chicken thigh on each bottom half, then 3 pickles, then the top bun.

Puli Inji Grilled Cheese

1 tablespoon unsalted butter,
    at room temperature
2 slices sourdough, thick-cut challah,
    or another bread of your choice
1 tablespoon Puli Inji (page 58)
2 slices Gouda, provolone,
    or Havarti cheese
Salt to taste

✳ **FREEZER NOTE**
Please don't freeze this sandwich.

The first thing I ever learned to cook for myself was a grilled cheese sandwich. I've made several hundred versions in my lifetime, and I've found that I've become more and more particular about how I like my grilled cheeses over the years. The best versions are built on either good sourdough or thick-cut slices of challah bread, grilled in butter (sorry, team mayo!), made with a good melty cheese that isn't American cheese, and spread with some sort of jam, pesto, or Indian pickle. If I have a batch of puli inji in my fridge, that is the first thing I reach for. Melty cheese pairs perfectly with the sweet-spicy-tangy flavor of the tamarind-ginger pickle. Sometimes, admittedly, I make puli inji just to make this grilled cheese. You just might, too.

Spread the butter on one side of each slice of bread and place them buttered side down on a work surface. Spread the puli inji across the two unbuttered sides. Layer the cheese on one piece of bread, then top with the remaining slice of bread, puli inji side down.

Heat a small skillet over medium heat. Place the sandwich in the skillet and sprinkle the top with a pinch of salt. Cook the sandwich for 2 to 3 minutes, until the bottom is golden and the cheese has started to melt. Flip the sandwich over, sprinkle the other side with a little bit of salt, and cook for another 2 minutes or so, until the bottom is golden and the cheese is completely melted. Transfer to a plate and cut in half (I prefer diagonally).

Bombay Grill Sandwiches

2 tablespoons unsalted butter,
    at room temperature

6 slices white sandwich or
    sourdough bread

3 tablespoons Cilantro-Mint
    Chutney (page 50)

2 slices mozzarella or provolone cheese

2 red potatoes, boiled, peeled,
    and thinly sliced

2 tablespoons Chaat Masala (page 63)

⅓ English cucumber, thinly sliced

2 Roma tomatoes, thinly sliced

½ medium red onion, thinly sliced

Ketchup, for dipping

❧ INGREDIENT NOTE

Traditionally, the sandwich is made with Amul cheese, a highly processed Indian cheese that is hard to find outside of an Indian grocery store. You can swap in another mild, sliceable white cheese like Gouda or provolone.

❄ FREEZER NOTE

Do not freeze.

There's something so charming about sandwiches with three slices of bread—it feels like you're breaking the rules and getting away with it. The Bombay grill sandwich is essentially a double-decker club sandwich, but with Indian flavors. The standard pile of cold cuts and bacon strips is replaced with a mound of vegetables like boiled potatoes, sliced cucumber, and onion. (Some like to add a layer of thinly cut cooked beets, too.) Mayonnaise is swapped out for cilantro chutney, and the whole thing is grilled at the end to gently melt the cheese and give the bread more texture. The sandwiches pair well with a pile of your favorite potato chips and a Shikanji Pimm's Cup (page 279).

Butter both sides of each piece of bread and place on a clean surface. Spread ½ tablespoon chutney on one side of each piece of bread. Add a slice of cheese on top of the chutney on 2 pieces of the bread. On those same pieces, divide and layer the potato slices. Add a generous sprinkle of chaat masala, then top each with another slice of bread, chutney side up. Add a layer of cucumber on top of the chutney, then sprinkle generously with chaat masala. Add a layer of tomatoes and onions and another generous sprinkling of chaat masala. Top with the remaining pieces of bread, chutney side down.

Heat a grill pan or large skillet over medium heat. Add the sandwiches and cook until the buttered bread is golden brown and the cheese is somewhat melted, about 3 minutes on each side. Cut in half and serve with ketchup for dipping.

DOSAS &

There are few dishes that better represent the differences between southern and northern Indian food than dosas and samosas—and not just because they rhyme. Dosas, made from a batter of fermented rice and lentils, are essentially Indian sourdough and a building block of south Indian cooking. Samosas, traditionally made with a tender and flaky wheat crust and potato filling, are a beloved snack from the north that lends itself well to innovation.

SAMOSAS

Jalapeño Popper Samosas

2 jalapeños, seeded and minced
  (see Ingredient Note)
6 ounces full-fat cream cheese,
  at room temperature
½ cup shredded mozzarella cheese
1 teaspoon Chaat Masala (page 63)
½ teaspoon salt
6 slices squishy white sandwich
  bread, crusts cut off
Neutral oil, for frying
Tamarind Chutney (page 52), for serving
Cilantro-Mint Chutney
  (page 50), for serving

❦ INGREDIENT NOTE

Keep the jalapeño seeds if you want more heat in your samosas. For those who want the jalapeño flavor but prefer a little less heat, you can swap in 12 or so pickled jalapeños for the raw peppers.

❅ FREEZER NOTE

These don't freeze very well, but that's okay! They are best consumed fresh.

The auntie superpower of being able to transform nearly everything into a samosa wrapper is unrivaled (apologies to the entire Marvel Cinematic Universe). Don't want to make the dough or don't have the ingredients? No problem. Use a tortilla! Or a dumpling wrapper! Or white sandwich bread! The method is shockingly effective. Cut the crusts off a piece of squishy-soft white bread, flatten it with a rolling pin, roll into a cone, fill, and fry and you have a golden and crunchy samosa. I've always imagined that jalapeño poppers should be made into a samosa—something about the creamy, spicy filling and a crispy crust just works so well. So the filling for these samosas contains cream cheese and jalapeños—and chaat masala, for good measure. These samosas are small, so be sure not to overstuff them.

In a small bowl, combine the jalapeños, cream cheese, mozzarella cheese, chaat masala, and salt. Mix until well combined.

Gently flatten each piece of bread with a rolling pin and then slice each piece in half on the diagonal to make 12 triangles. Pick up one triangle and use a bit of water on your fingertip to dampen the edges. Roll the triangle into a cone and make sure the point of the cone is sealed using water and your fingers to press it together. Stuff the samosa with ½ tablespoon of the filling, then fold over the remaining edge, using your fingers dipped in water to press the edges together to seal. Make sure to seal well or the cheese could ooze out. Repeat with the remaining triangles and filling.

Pour 2 to 3 inches of oil into a large pot and heat until it hits 275 degrees F. Drop 4 samosas in at a time and fry until they are golden brown on the outside and gooey and melty on the inside, 1 to 2 minutes. Drain the samosas on a plate lined with paper towels. Repeat to fry the remaining samosas. Serve hot, but bite into them with caution. Use the chutneys for dipping.

Samosa Pinwheels

2 tablespoons neutral oil

2 teaspoons cumin seeds

½ medium white onion, diced

1 green serrano pepper, seeded and minced

1 tablespoon ginger paste *or* 1–inch piece fresh ginger, grated

1 cup frozen green peas, thawed

4 small red potatoes *or* 1 large russet potato, boiled, peeled, and diced

¼ cup chopped fresh cilantro

2 teaspoons salt

2 teaspoons ground coriander

2 teaspoons Garam Masala (page 62)

2 teaspoons Chaat Masala (page 63)

1 teaspoon amchur

1 teaspoon Kashmiri red chili powder

All-purpose flour, for dusting

1 sheet puff pastry, thawed according to package instructions

Tamarind Chutney (page 52), for serving

Cilantro-Mint Chutney (page 50), for serving

❧ INGREDIENT NOTE

Different brands of frozen puff pastry take a different amount of time to cook and puff up, so keep your eye on the samosa pinwheels and add or decrease oven time as needed. I tested this recipe with my favorite frozen puff pastry brand, Pepperidge Farm.

✳ FREEZER NOTE

Leftover samosa pinwheels freeze well when wrapped in aluminum foil and stored in an airtight container for 1 to 2 months. To reheat, bake at 300 degrees F until warmed through.

I am so thankful for the frozen section of the supermarket and its bounty of puff pastry. It means there's a no-fry option available when I want to eat samosas or make an appetizer for a dinner party that will impress with minimal effort. These pinwheels, which are so flaky and tender, are stuffed with a traditional samosa filling and then baked until the super buttery puff pastry is crisp and golden brown—no vat of oil required. Just make sure to properly thaw the puff pastry (see Ingredient Note) or the pinwheels will be impossible to roll up.

Preheat the oven to 400 degrees F. Line a rimmed baking sheet with parchment paper.

Heat the oil in a large nonstick skillet over medium heat. Add the cumin seeds and once they start to sizzle and jump, add the onion and serrano pepper and cook for 2 to 3 minutes, until soft. Add the ginger and peas and cook for another minute or so, then transfer the mixture to a large bowl and let cool slightly.

Add the potatoes, cilantro, salt, coriander, garam masala, chaat masala, amchur, and chili powder to the bowl with the onion mixture. Mix well, but don't fully mash the potatoes (I like to keep a little texture).

Sprinkle some flour on a work surface and roll out the thawed puff pastry into a thinner rectangle, about 20 percent larger than the original sheet. Spread the potato mixture evenly over the puff pastry, leaving a ¼-inch border on both of the shorter sides. Roll the puff pastry up like a log, starting from one of the longer sides. Using your sharpest knife, or a piece of unflavored dental floss, cut the log into ½-inch-thick rounds. Place the rounds cut side down on the prepared baking sheet, making sure to keep a little space between them. Bake for 12 to 15 minutes, until puffy and golden. Let the pinwheels cool for 5 minutes, then serve with bowls of chutney for dipping.

JALAPEÑO POPPER
SAMOSAS

CLASSIC PUNJABI
SAMOSAS

COCKTAIL PIZZA SAMOSAS

SAMOSA PINWHEELS

Cocktail Pizza Samosas

½ cup finely chopped bell pepper
(any color you like)

½ cup finely chopped white onion

6 black olives, pitted and sliced

3 tablespoons frozen corn,
thawed (optional)

¼ cup marinara sauce

2 cups shredded mozzarella cheese

1 teaspoon salt

½ teaspoon Chaat Masala (page 63)

½ teaspoon Italian seasoning

¼ teaspoon ground black pepper

1 tablespoon all-purpose flour

1 tablespoon water

6 spring roll wrappers

Neutral oil, for frying

Ranch, barbecue sauce, or Cilantro-
Mint Chutney (page 50), for dipping

❄ FREEZER NOTE

These are best eaten hot out of the fryer.
Don't freeze.

🍴 EXTRA CREDIT

You can customize your fillings and include
pepperoni, sausage, or even drained
canned pineapple.

Here "cocktail" refers to the size of the samosa, not the inclusion of booze. They are party-sized and are one of the best appetizers in the game. Unlike Punjabi-style samosas, which are much heftier in size, you can eat several of these without filling up completely. Cocktail samosas also tend to have a thinner crust, which is why I like to use spring roll wrappers for this recipe.

I stuffed all the toppings I love on a veggie supreme–style pizza into this recipe.

In a small bowl, combine the bell pepper, onion, olives, corn (if using), marinara, cheese, salt, chaat masala, Italian seasoning, and black pepper. In another small bowl, whisk together the flour and water to create a thick paste with no lumps. You will use this to seal the samosas.

Stack the spring roll wrappers and slice them in half on the diagonal, to make two triangles each. Place one triangle so that the longest side is parallel to your work surface. Take the right corner and fold it over so that it hits the middle point of the left side and press down. Now take the left corner, brushing paste on the side facing you, and fold it to the right, so that it lines up with the corner of the first fold. Press down to seal. Make sure the point of the cone is well sealed!

Pick up the folded wrapper and hold it so that the cone point faces down and the opening faces up. Fill the samosa with about 1 tablespoon of the filling. Fold the two excess hanging corners in toward the center of the samosa, then brush the flour mixture on the remaining triangle. Fold the triangle over the filling, making sure that every edge is sealed and all three corners are somewhat pointy. Repeat with the remaining wrappers and filling.

Pour a few inches of oil into a large pot or deep skillet and heat to 275 degrees F. Working in batches as necessary, fry the samosas until they are golden brown, 3 to 4 minutes. Drain on a paper towel–lined plate.

Basic Plain Dosas

1½ cups long-grain white rice

½ cup urad dal (whole or split)

½ teaspoon fenugreek seeds
   (optional; see Ingredient Note)

Water, as needed

1 tablespoon salt

Neutral oil, for cooking

❦ INGREDIENT NOTE

The fenugreek seeds (also known as methi seeds) are not crucial to the recipe, but my mom swears they don't only enhance flavor but also help with fermentation. I poked into the science and it turns out fenugreek seeds contain compounds high in beta-glucans, which help the batter hold onto carbon dioxide, which in turn helps make the batter bubbly.

❄ FREEZER NOTE

You can freeze dosa batter in an airtight container for up to 3 months. Just let it thaw in the fridge before using it. Don't freeze cooked dosas.

Dosas are often compared to crepes (and even though I find that reductive, I can see why), but dosa is actually Indian sourdough. They may be cooked like crepes, in a thin circular layer on a flat pan, but the batter is made from a mix of lentils and rice that is fermented until super tangy, bubbly, and just the right amount of sour. Fermentation is the trickiest part of making dosa batter, but my mom's method makes it significantly easier. She taught me to keep the batter in the oven with only the light on—you just have to adjust the time needed depending on the temperature of your kitchen. The colder it is, the longer it could take.

Though dosas are thought of as more of a breakfast food in south India, in the American diaspora, they are more commonly served for lunch or dinner. I love going out to a restaurant for a great crispy dosa, and having it show up to the table the same length as an NBA player's wingspan. (The dosas in this recipe are much more manageable in size.)

Dosas are best served with bowls of Sambar (page 131) and lots of Coconut Chutney (page 56). You can wrap dosas around a filling of spiced potatoes called Dosa Masala (page 124), though I prefer to eat the potatoes on the side. Dosas are also delicious sprinkled with Gunpowder Chutney (page 57), or with some more nontraditional fillings like maple and butter, green chiles and cheese, or garlic and parmesan (see variations). Best of all, any leftover batter can be transformed into Uttapam (page 129).

Recipe continues

Combine the rice, dal, and fenugreek seeds (if using) in a large bowl. Rinse and drain the rice mixture 2 or 3 times to rinse off the starches. Fill the bowl back up with water so that there is an inch covering the rice and soak for at least 8 hours or up to 24 hours. I like to soak it overnight and make the batter in the morning.

Drain the water and transfer the rice and lentils to a blender. Add fresh water to the blender until the mixture is covered. Blend until everything is finely ground—it should look like thin pancake batter.

Pour the batter into a large container, cover, and leave to ferment in a warm but not hot spot. I find the easiest way to do this is to place the batter in the oven with the light turned on (*not* the oven itself) for at least 12 hours. The batter is ready when it is bubbly, frothy, and has that eau de fermentation—a slightly funky, tangy scent. (This could take longer depending on how cold your kitchen is.) Unlike typical yeasted breads, do not expect the dosa batter to totally double in size (though it will grow). Add the salt and mix well. You want the batter to be pourable but not runny; you can add a little water if it's too thick or a pinch of Cream of Wheat if it's too thin.

Heat a small nonstick skillet over high heat. Sprinkle a few drops of water on the pan, and if they immediately bubble up and quickly evaporate then the pan is hot enough. Pour a small drop of neutral oil in the pan and carefully use a wadded-up paper towel to spread the oil around the pan. Pour ¼ cup of the batter into the pan in concentric circles to spread out the batter, starting from the center and moving outward. Use the back of a ladle to help spread the batter, going in a circular motion, working from the center outward. Drizzle a few drops of oil over the dosa as it is cooking. Turn the heat up to medium-high and cook until the bottom of the dosa is light brown (or medium brown if you like it crispier), then fold the dosa in half and slide it onto a plate using a spatula. The center is generally softer and thicker, while the outer edges tend to be a little bit thinner and crispier. Repeat the process until you're sick of making dosas (I find it meditative!), everyone is full, or you're out of batter.

MAPLE SEA SALT DOSA

For this sweet-and-salty breakfast-inspired dosa, don't fold the dosa in half once it's cooked. Pull it off the heat and add 1 pat good butter to the center. Drizzle with 1 teaspoon maple syrup and sprinkle with a pinch of flaky sea salt. Fold the dosa in half before serving.

CHILE CHEESE DOSA

This wonderfully gooey dosa is inspired by a variation found on the menu at Paper Dosa in Santa Fe, made with Hatch chiles. As the dosa is cooking, sprinkle it evenly with ¼ cup shredded Colby jack or cheddar cheese, then evenly distribute 4 to 6 pickled jalapeños or 1 teaspoon drained canned diced Hatch chiles. Fold the dosa in half before serving.

GARLIC BREAD DOSA

I believe garlic makes basically everything better, including dosas. Mix together 1½ teaspoons softened butter, 1 minced garlic clove, and a scattering of minced fresh parsley leaves. Spread the butter mixture on the cooked dosa, then sprinkle evenly with grated parmesan cheese. Fold in half before serving.

Dosa Masala

5 tablespoons neutral oil, divided

2 medium yellow onions, thinly sliced

2 tablespoons urad dal

¾ cup cashew pieces

9 or 10 red potatoes, boiled, peeled, and cut into ¼-inch pieces

2 green serrano peppers, diced

2 teaspoons salt

1½ teaspoons ground turmeric

5 tablespoons water

🥣 STORAGE NOTE

Do not freeze the dosa masala. It will keep well in an airtight container in the fridge for up to 5 days.

🍴 EXTRA CREDIT

I like to crisp up leftover dosa masala in a pan with a bit of oil and serve them instead of homefries or hash browns. Especially great when topped with a fried egg.

If you ever order a masala dosa at a restaurant, it will arrive hot and crispy, rolled around a filling of soft, spicy potatoes (known as the masala). I find that restaurant versions are often too mushy or watery and generally lacking in nuanced flavors and textures. But when done right, the masala can be the difference between a good dosa experience and an ethereal dosa experience. This version, taught to me by my mom, features gently caramelized onions that add a hit of sweetness, cashews and urad dal for bite, and potatoes that are tender but not gloopy. I love this potato recipe so much that I often eat it by itself—no dosa necessary.

Heat 4 tablespoons oil in a large skillet over medium heat. Add the onions and sauté for 4 to 5 minutes, until the onions soften and start to take on color. Push the onions to one side of the pan and add the remaining 1 tablespoon oil. Add the urad dal to the oil and fry for 30 to 60 seconds, until it browns. Add the cashew pieces and let them brown, 30 to 60 seconds. Add the potatoes, serrano peppers, salt, and turmeric and mix everything together. Add the water and let it cook for another 2 to 3 minutes.

Rava Dosas

½ cup semolina flour or Cream of Wheat

½ cup rice flour

¼ cup all-purpose flour

2 tablespoons plain full-fat yogurt

3½ cups water, divided

1 red onion, diced

1 green serrano pepper, diced

2 tablespoon chopped fresh cilantro

1 teaspoon ginger paste
    or ¼-piece fresh ginger, grated

10 to 12 fresh or dried curry
    leaves (optional)

2 teaspoons cumin seeds

1½ teaspoons salt

1 teaspoon ground black pepper

Neutral oil, for cooking

The problem with making Basic Plain Dosas (page 121) is that it requires planning ahead. This is where rava dosas, made with semolina flour (also known as sooji or rava) and rice flour, come in handy. They require zero fermentation, and the batter comes together quickly. A rava dosa is essentially one big, lacy, crispy disk. The lacey pattern is a signature characteristic, and the only way to achieve it is with an extremely thin, almost watery batter. Learning to pour the batter properly to achieve that lacey pattern can be tricky, but it gets easier with practice. Rava dosas pair well with Sambar (page 131), Coconut Chutney (page 56), and my favorite almost-chutney: ketchup.

In a large bowl, combine the semolina flour, rice flour, and all-purpose flour and mix well. Add the yogurt and 2 cups water and whisk until a smooth batter forms. You want the batter to be the consistency and color of buttermilk.

Mix the onion, serrano pepper, cilantro, ginger, and curry leaves (if using) into the batter. Stir until evenly mixed, then stir in the cumin seeds, salt, and black pepper. Add another ½ cup water to the batter to make sure it is thin. Let the batter sit for 15 minutes. This allows the Cream of Wheat to absorb the liquid and soften, which helps create the ideal rava dosa texture.

Stir the batter again, as there will be stuff that settles to the bottom. Add the remaining 1 cup water. You want the batter to be super thin—as thin as the consistency of milk. This batter is extremely watery! Do not be alarmed.

Recipe continues

Heat a large nonstick or cast-iron skillet over high heat. Once the pan is hot (you can test this by dropping a little water on the pan; it will bubble immediately), add a little oil and use a wadded-up paper towel to coat the pan. Use a cup with a spout to pour in enough batter to coat the bottom of the pan. You want to pour from up high (about 6 inches above the pan) so that you can create the lacy pattern. This takes a little bit of practice. It's easiest to pour the batter on the outer edge of the pan and work your way in. The key is to never go back over the areas in which you've already poured batter.

Let the dosa cook for 1 to 2 minutes, until the bottom starts to turn golden. Drizzle a little oil over the dosa and let it cook for another minute or so. Use a spatula to loosen the edges of the dosa. It should feel nice and crisp but still pliable. Fold the dosa in half and slide it onto a plate. Repeat until you've run out of batter, adding more oil as needed.

Uttapam

2 cups batter for Basic Plain
    Dosas (page 121)
½ red onion, minced
½ green serrano pepper, minced
½ medium tomato, diced
⅓ cup finely chopped fresh cilantro
1 tablespoon ginger paste *or* 1-inch
    piece fresh ginger, grated
½ teaspoon salt
Neutral oil, for cooking

✳ FREEZER NOTE

Cooked uttapam can be frozen in an air-tight container for up to 3 months if separated by parchment paper and wrapped tightly. To reheat, thaw at room temperature and heat up in a pan.

My personal hero is whoever figured out that dosa batter could also be transformed into thick, savory pancakes. Throw a handful of diced or shredded vegetables into the batter—I like onions, tomatoes, cilantro, and serrano peppers—and then cook it as you would a buttermilk pancake, and suddenly you have an uttapam. Like dosas, uttapam taste great with a side of Sambar (page 131) and Coconut Chutney (page 56). I add a third side: a generous squirt of Heinz ketchup. Make sure to cook the uttapam in enough oil so that it achieves those great crispy, lacey edges. I've also seen people pour uttapam batter into a waffle maker, if you're feeling inspired.

In a medium bowl, combine the dosa batter, onion, serrano pepper, tomato, cilantro, ginger, and salt and mix well.

Heat a little oil in a small nonstick skillet over medium heat. Pour about ½ cup of the batter into the pan and cook the first side for 2 to 3 minutes, until it starts to crisp up and gently brown. Flip the pancake and cook the other side for 2 to 3 minutes, then slide it onto a plate. Repeat with the remaining batter, adding more oil as needed.

SAMBAR

KETCHUP

UTTAPAM

SERVES 4

Sambar

SAMBAR

½ cup toor dal (split yellow pigeon peas), rinsed
2 ½ cups water, divided
2 ounces frozen drumsticks (optional; see Ingredient Note)
1 ½ teaspoons ginger paste *or* ½-inch piece fresh ginger, grated
1 teaspoon salt
½ teaspoon ground turmeric
½ teaspoon Kashmiri red chili powder
Juice of ½ lemon

TADKA

1 tablespoon neutral oil or ghee
½ teaspoon black mustard seeds
15 fresh curry leaves (optional)
1 ½ Roma tomatoes, diced
2 teaspoons sambar masala (see Ingredient Note)

🌿 **INGREDIENT NOTE**

Drumsticks, also known as moringa, can be found in the frozen aisle of most Indian stores, and are completely optional. If you can't find a premade sambar masala in stores or online (I like MDH brand), you can substitute 1 ½ teaspoons Garam Masala (page 62), ¼ teaspoon ground cumin, and ¼ teaspoon ground coriander as a quick fix.

❄️ **FREEZER NOTE**

I love freezing batches of sambar. It will keep in an airtight container in the freezer for up to 4 months. To reheat, use a microwave or stovetop; no need to thaw.

Sambar is a staple of South Indian cooking (and the name of my favorite group chat) and has the slurpable texture of soup—but to call sambar "lentil soup" is doing it a disservice. Yes, you could eat a bowl of sambar on its own, but it's magical when paired with a scoop of white rice or served with a Basic Plain Dosa (page 121) or Uttapam (page 129) for dunking. I keep my sambar simple and on the brothy side, but you can easily add more vegetables, such as carrots, potatoes, or eggplant—just toss them in with the drumsticks.

Combine the toor dal and 1 ½ cups water in an Instant Pot and cook on high pressure for 9 minutes, until the dal is soft.

Pour the cooked lentils and their liquid into a large, heavy-bottomed pot and add the remaining 1 cup water. Blend the dal using an immersion blender until it is smooth. (Alternatively, you can use a regular countertop blender.) Turn the heat to medium and add the drumsticks (if using), ginger, salt, turmeric, and chili powder.

To make the tadka, in a small saucepan, heat the oil over medium-high heat. Add the mustard seeds and let them pop. Turn the heat down to low, add the curry leaves (if using), and cook for about 10 seconds. Add the diced tomatoes, stir, and turn the heat up to medium-high. Let the tomatoes cook for about 3 minutes, stirring occasionally. Remove the pan from the heat, add the sambar masala, and give it a good stir. Add the tadka and lemon juice to the pot with the lentils, mix well, and bring to a boil. Turn down the heat and let it simmer, uncovered, for 20 minutes.

131

In 1986, Dalvinder Multani, an Indian immigrant who had spent time making pizza in New York City, purchased an old pizzeria in San Francisco called Zante's. He opened an Indian restaurant in the space but continued to sell pizzas, too. A customer kept asking him to combine the two—north Indian classics like tandoori chicken with the cheesy, saucy, miracle that is pizza—creating one of the most delicious innovations to date. Today, several Indian pizza shops can be found around the country, but the best one might just be your own kitchen.

PIZZA

PARTY

Basic Indian Pizza Dough

⅔ cup lukewarm water

1 tablespoon honey

1½ teaspoons active dry yeast

2 tablespoons olive oil, plus
     more for greasing

1¾ cups all-purpose flour

1 teaspoon salt

1 teaspoon cumin seeds, toasted

1 teaspoon kalonji (nigella seeds; optional)

❄ FREEZER NOTE
Lightly coat the dough with oil, then place it in a ziplock bag. Press the air out of the bag, then seal tightly and freeze for up to 3 months. Thaw in the fridge.

There are many incredible pizza dough recipes, but most of them require waiting for the dough to rise at least overnight, which doesn't work for me. This dough takes only 1½ to 2 hours to rise! You do need to wait for it to double in size—which means that if you suddenly want pizza at lunch, it can easily happen at dinner. I spiked the dough with cumin and nigella seeds to give it more dimension. And even with the short rise time, it yields a surprisingly pillowy crust. That being said, if you like to plan ahead, you can make this dough the night before and let it rise in the fridge overnight.

In a medium bowl, whisk together the water, honey, and yeast, then let it sit for 5 minutes. It should be foamy (if it's not, it means your yeast is dead and you need to get fresh yeast and start over). Add the olive oil and give the mixture a good stir. Add the flour, salt, cumin seeds, and kalonji (if using). Using a wooden spoon, mix everything together until a shaggy dough forms. Knead the dough in the bowl using your hands for about 2 minutes, making sure there are no floury spots left on the dough. Shape the dough into a ball and transfer to a lightly oiled bowl. Cover and let it rise in a warm spot for 1½ hours to 2 hours, until it is doubled in size. Now use it to make any of the pizza recipes that follow.

Achari Paneer Pizza

PANEER

¼ cup plain full-fat yogurt

2 tablespoons achar of your choice (see Ingredient Note)

4 ounces paneer, cut into ½- to 1-inch cubes

CREAMY TOMATO SAUCE

1 teaspoon olive oil

½ medium white onion, minced

1 tablespoon garlic paste
   or 3 garlic cloves, minced

½ cup tomato puree

1 teaspoon Kashmiri red chili powder

1 teaspoon Garam Masala (page 62)

½ teaspoon salt

1 teaspoon kasoori methi or dried oregano

½ teaspoon sugar

PIZZA

All-purpose flour, for dusting

½ recipe Basic Indian Pizza Dough (page 135)

Olive oil, for drizzling

½ to 1 cup shredded mozzarella cheese (Shred it yourself! Pre-shredded has fillers and doesn't always melt.)

¼ red onion, thinly sliced

8 to 10 pickled jalapeños (optional)

Fresh cilantro leaves, for garnish (optional)

Little tastes better on pizza than paneer, but it must be done right. People forget that paneer is essentially the tofu of the cheese world, in that it is incredible at soaking up flavors applied to it but doesn't have the strongest flavor on its own. Tossing the paneer pieces in a marinade of yogurt and your favorite achar (see Ingredient Note) yields magic, especially when combined with a slightly sweet and wonderfully garlicky Indian-y tomato sauce.

In a medium bowl, combine the yogurt and achar and stir until well combined. Add the paneer cubes and toss until well coated. Cover and refrigerate for at least 30 minutes.

Preheat the oven to 450 degrees F. Place a rimmed baking sheet on the lower rack of the oven.

Meanwhile, make the tomato sauce. Heat the oil in a medium saucepan over medium heat. Add the onion and sauté until soft, about 3 minutes. Add the garlic and cook for another 30 seconds or so, then add the tomato puree. Let cook for another minute or two, stirring constantly. The sauce should thicken a little. Add the chili powder, garam masala, and salt, give it a good stir, and cook for another minute. Stir in the kasoori methi and sugar. Turn off the heat. (If not using right away, let cool, cover, and refrigerate for up to 3 days.)

On a lightly floured work surface, use your hands to gently stretch out the dough. You want it to be 6 to 8 inches in diameter. Remove the baking sheet from the oven and drizzle it with olive oil, which will lightly sizzle, then place the stretched-out dough on the oiled pan. Bake for about 8 minutes, until the crust is mostly cooked through but still light in color.

✤ INGREDIENT NOTE

Achars are fruits and vegetables that are pickled with oil and spices. You could make your own, but it's a lot of effort, and they are readily available at any Indian grocery store. I am partial to a spicy mango achar, or the roasted garlic achar from Brooklyn Delhi (which is available at most Whole Foods).

❄ FREEZER NOTE

You can wrap leftover pizza in aluminum foil, place in a ziplock bag, and freeze for up to 1 month. Reheat in the oven. Don't microwave your pizza, please. You can also freeze any leftover tomato sauce in an air-tight container for up to 2 months; thaw in the fridge before using.

Remove from the oven and top evenly with the tomato sauce, then the mozzarella cheese, marinated paneer cubes, red onion slices, and pickled jalapeños (if using). Return the pizza to the oven and bake until the cheese melts, another 3 minutes or so. Top with cilantro (if using) and, once the pizza has somewhat cooled, slice and serve.

ACHARI PANEER PIZZA
(PAGE 136)

CHEESY MASALA CORN
PIZZA (PAGE 145)

GREEN CHUTNEY
PIZZA (PAGE 147)

SAMOSA PIZZA (PAGE 142)

Tandoori Vegetable Supreme Pizza

TANDOORI VEGETABLES

½ cup plain full-fat yogurt

2 teaspoons garlic paste
   or 2 garlic cloves, minced

2 teaspoons ginger paste *or* ½-inch
   piece fresh ginger, grated

½ teaspoon amchur

½ teaspoon ground cumin

½ teaspoon Kashmiri red chili powder

½ teaspoon salt

½ teaspoon ground black pepper

¼ teaspoon ground cardamom

½ cup halved cremini mushrooms

4 to 6 broccoli florets

¼ red onion, thinly sliced

⅓ red bell pepper, cut into strips

CREAMY TOMATO SAUCE

1 teaspoon olive oil

½ medium white onion, minced

1 tablespoon garlic paste
   or 3 garlic cloves, minced

½ cup tomato puree

1 teaspoon Kashmiri red chili powder

1 teaspoon Garam Masala (page 62)

½ teaspoon salt

1 teaspoon kasoori methi or dried oregano

½ teaspoon sugar

I love a pizza place that offers a vegetable supreme pizza loaded with basically every vegetable on the menu: Mushrooms! Onions! Broccoli! Bell peppers! (I tell myself it's essentially a salad . . . but pizza.) I am also convinced that basically every vegetable tastes better when you cook it tandoori style (marinated in yogurt and spices). So why not combine the two into one glorious pizza? If you're short on time or generally uninterested in measuring out spices, feel free to replace the dried spices with 1 tablespoon premade tandoori masala.

In a medium bowl, combine the yogurt, garlic, ginger, amchur, cumin, chili powder, salt, black pepper, and cardamom. Add the mushrooms, broccoli, red onion, and bell pepper and mix until the vegetables are well coated. Cover the bowl and refrigerate for at least 1 hour.

While the veggies are in the fridge, make the tomato sauce. Heat the oil in a medium saucepan over medium heat. Add the onion and sauté until soft, about 3 minutes. Add the garlic and cook for another 30 seconds or so, then add the tomato puree. Let cook for another minute or two, stirring constantly. The sauce should thicken a little. Add the chili powder, garam masala, and salt, give it a good stir, and cook for another minute. Stir in the kasoori methi and sugar. Turn off the heat. (If not using right away, let cool, cover, and refrigerate for up to 3 days.)

Preheat the oven to 375 degrees F. Line a rimmed baking sheet with parchment paper.

PIZZA

All-purpose flour, for dusting

½ recipe Basic Indian Pizza
    Dough (page 135)

Olive oil, for drizzling

½ to 1 cup shredded mozzarella cheese
    (Shred it yourself! Pre-shredded has
    fillers and doesn't always melt.)

1 tablespoon kasoori methi (optional)

❄ FREEZER NOTE

You can wrap leftover pizza in aluminum foil, place in a ziplock bag, and freeze for up to 1 month. Reheat in the oven. Don't microwave your pizza, please.

Spread out the yogurt-marinated vegetables on the prepared baking sheet and roast for 8 to 10 minutes, until the vegetables are cooked through. Set aside.

Turn the oven up to 450 degrees F. Place another rimmed baking sheet on the lower rack of the oven and let it heat up for 10 minutes.

On a floured surface, use your hands to gently stretch out the dough. You want it to be 6 to 8 inches in diameter. Remove the baking sheet from the oven and drizzle it with olive oil, which will lightly sizzle, then place the stretched-out dough on the oiled pan. Bake for about 8 minutes, until the crust is mostly cooked through but still light in color.

Remove from the oven and top evenly with the tomato sauce, then the shredded mozzarella cheese and the tandoori roasted vegetables. Return the pizza to the oven and bake until the cheese melts, another 3 minutes or so. Sprinkle with the kasoori methi, if you like. Once the pizza has somewhat cooled, slice and serve.

Samosa Pizza

DESI TOMATO SAUCE

1 teaspoon olive oil

½ small white onion, minced

1 tablespoon garlic paste
   or 3 garlic cloves, minced

½ cup tomato puree

1 tablespoon Garam Masala (page 62)

½ teaspoon salt

SAMOSA TOPPING

1 tablespoon olive oil

2 or 3 small red potatoes or 1 large
   russet potato, boiled, peeled,
   and cut into ½-inch cubes

½ green serrano pepper, minced

1 teaspoon ground cumin

1 teaspoon ground coriander

½ teaspoon Garam Masala (page 62)

½ teaspoon salt

¼ teaspoon ground turmeric

Juice of ½ lemon

Samosa pizza is quite different from Cocktail Pizza Samosas (see page 120), but it solidifies the fact that the samosa and pizza are basically besties. This pizza is so much more than taking a samosa, chopping it up, throwing it on a crust with some sauce and cheese, and calling it a day. Instead, each part of the samosa is separated out, so that the result still tastes like samosa, but feels like pizza. The potatoes are cooked and tossed with spices, the peas are scattered and separated, the pizza base acts like the samosa crust, and the chutneys get swirled on top. Don't skip the addition of the pickled jalapeños or the cilantro—they will brighten up each pie.

Preheat the oven to 450 degrees F. Place a rimmed baking sheet on the lower rack of the oven.

To make the tomato sauce, in a medium saucepan, heat the olive oil over medium heat. Add the onion and sauté until soft, about 3 minutes. Stir in the garlic and cook for 30 seconds. Pour in the tomato puree, then stir in the garam masala and salt. Let the sauce heat through and slightly thicken, stirring occasionally, for 3 minutes. Remove from the heat.

To make the samosa topping, in a Dutch oven or other large, heavy-bottomed pot, heat the oil over medium heat. Add the potatoes and serrano pepper and cook, stirring, for 1 minute. Add the cumin, coriander, garam masala, salt, and turmeric and stir until everything is well coated. Add the lemon juice, toss to coat, and remove from the heat.

PIZZA

All-purpose flour, for dusting

½ recipe Basic Indian Pizza
    Dough (page 135)

Olive oil, for drizzling

½ to 1 cup shredded mozzarella cheese
    (Shred it yourself! Pre-shredded has
    fillers and doesn't always melt.)

½ cup frozen green peas, thawed

8 to 10 slices pickled jalapeño (optional)

Fresh cilantro leaves, for garnish

Tamarind Chutney (page 52),
    for drizzling (optional)

Cilantro-Mint Chutney (page 50),
    for drizzling (optional)

❄ FREEZER NOTE

You can wrap leftover pizza in aluminum foil, place in a ziplock bag, and freeze for up to 4 weeks. Reheat in the oven. Don't microwave your pizza, please.

On a lightly floured work surface, use your hands to gently stretch out the dough. You want it to be 6 to 8 inches in diameter. Remove the baking sheet from the oven and drizzle it with olive oil, which will lightly sizzle, then place the stretched-out dough on the oiled pan. Bake for about 8 minutes, until the crust is mostly cooked through but still light in color.

Remove from the oven and top evenly with the tomato sauce, then the shredded mozzarella cheese, spiced potatoes, peas, and pickled jalapeños, if using. Return the pizza to the oven and bake until the cheese melts, another 3 minutes or so. Top with fresh cilantro and drizzle with the chutneys, if using—I like to swirl the chutneys for aesthetics! Once the pizza has somewhat cooled, slice and serve.

Cheesy Masala Corn Pizza

MASALA CORN

2 teaspoons unsalted butter

1 cup fresh or frozen sweet corn
    kernels, cooked (though fresh
    would also taste great)

1 tablespoon lemon juice

1 teaspoon Kashmiri red chili powder

1 teaspoon Chaat Masala (page 63)

½ teaspoon ground cumin

½ teaspoon salt

Ground black pepper to taste

BÉCHAMEL

2 tablespoons unsalted butter

1 tablespoon all-purpose flour

⅔ cup whole milk

½ teaspoon salt

Black pepper to taste

2 tablespoons shredded mozzarella

PIZZA

All-purpose flour, for dusting

½ recipe Basic Indian Pizza
    Dough (page 135)

Olive oil, for drizzling

½ to 1 cup shredded mozzarella cheese
    (Shred it yourself! Pre-shredded has
    fillers and doesn't always melt.)

8 to 10 slices pickled jalapeño (optional)

Fresh cilantro leaves, for garnish (optional)

One of my core memories is running around Ahmedabad, the city in India where my family is from, on the back of my cousin Sagar's scooter. We were idiot teenagers who liked to run off and smoke too much hookah and try all the street food that I, as a visitor from America with a gentle digestive system, was not supposed to be eating. But Sagar always knew the best spots and who was I to deny my culinary heritage?

One night, he took me to a roadside cart that sold only one thing: cups of masala corn. Gently charred corn kernels, sliced off the cob, get tossed with a generous amount of butter, plenty of lemon juice, and lots of chaat masala and Kashmiri red chili powder. The only choice you had was to either have the corn showered with thinly shredded cheese or not. I obviously opted for the cheese. This is my homage to one of the best things I've ever eaten, reimagined as a pizza.

Preheat the oven to 450 degrees F. Place a rimmed baking sheet on the lower rack of the oven.

To make the masala corn, melt the butter in a large skillet over medium heat. Add the corn and stir so that each kernel is well coated in butter. Stir in the lemon juice, chili powder, chaat masala, cumin, salt, and black pepper and cook for 1 to 2 minutes. Remove the pan from the heat.

To make the béchamel, in a small saucepan, melt the butter over medium heat. Add the flour and whisk until the roux turns golden brown. Add the milk slowly, whisking until the sauce thickens, 1 to 2 minutes. Season with the salt and pepper and fold in the cheese. Give it a good mix and remove from the heat.

Recipe continues

On a lightly floured work surface, use your hands to gently stretch out the dough. You want it to be 6 to 8 inches in diameter. Remove the baking sheet from the oven and drizzle it with olive oil, which will lightly sizzle, then place the stretched-out dough on the oiled pan. Bake for about 8 minutes, until the crust is mostly cooked through but still light in color.

Remove from the oven and top evenly with the béchamel, then the shredded mozzarella cheese, then the masala corn. Return the pizza to the oven and bake until the cheese melts, another 3 minutes or so. Serve hot with pickled jalapeños and cilantro, if using.

Green Chutney Pizza

BÉCHAMEL

2 tablespoons unsalted butter

1 tablespoon all-purpose flour

⅔ cup whole milk

½ teaspoon salt

Black pepper to taste

2 tablespoons shredded mozzarella

PIZZA

All-purpose flour, for dusting

½ recipe Basic Indian Pizza
   Dough (page 135)

Olive oil, for drizzling

½ to 1 cup shredded mozzarella cheese
   (Shred it yourself! Pre-shredded has
   fillers and doesn't always melt.)

¼ red onion, thinly sliced (optional)

½ cup Cilantro-Mint Chutney (page 50)

❋ FREEZER NOTE

You can wrap leftover pizza in aluminum foil, place in a ziplock bag, and freeze for up to 1 month. Reheat in the oven. Don't microwave your pizza, please.

I love a white pizza. It always feels a little mischievous as an adult to eat a slice that doesn't have tomato sauce, especially when there are no other vegetables on the pizza. But sometimes tomato sauce is too dominant of a flavor, and I love the way using a béchamel as a sauce lets the flavor of the green chutney shine. This white pizza is gently inspired by one of my favorite pizzas at Rubirosa in New York City, where they top the pizza with fresh mozzarella and a glorious giant swirl of verdant pesto. Why not try it with a great, fresh cilantro chutney?

Preheat the oven to 450 degrees F. Place a rimmed baking sheet on the lower rack of the oven.

To make the béchamel, in a small saucepan, melt the butter over medium heat. Add the flour and whisk until the roux turns golden brown. Add the milk slowly, whisking until the sauce thickens, 1 to 2 minutes. Season with the salt and pepper and fold in the cheese. Give it a good mix, then remove from the heat.

On a lightly floured surface, use your hands to gently stretch out the dough. You want it to be 6 to 8 inches in diameter. Remove the baking sheet from the oven and drizzle it with olive oil, which will lightly sizzle, then place the stretched-out dough on the oiled pan. Bake for about 8 minutes, until the crust is mostly cooked through but still light in color.

Remove from the oven and top evenly with the béchamel, then the shredded mozzarella cheese and red onion, if using. Return the pizza to the oven and bake until the cheese melts, another 3 minutes or so. Top with the chutney—you can drizzle it with a spoon or make little dollops all over the pizza. I prefer to pour it into a squeeze bottle and make a swirl over the whole pizza, starting at the center and working my way out. Once the pizza has somewhat cooled, slice and serve.

Butter Chicken Pizza

½ cup Classic Butter Chicken,
    chilled (page 188)

All-purpose flour, for dusting

½ recipe Basic Indian Pizza
    Dough (page 135)

Olive oil, for drizzling

½ to 1 cup shredded mozzarella cheese
    (Shred it yourself! Pre-shredded has
    fillers and doesn't always melt.)

¼ small red onion, thinly sliced

4 to 8 pickled jalapeños (optional)

Small handful fresh cilantro
    leaves, chopped

2 to 3 fresh mint leaves,
    chopped (optional)

❄ **FREEZER NOTE**
You can wrap leftover pizza in aluminum foil, place in a ziplock bag, and freeze for up to 4 weeks. Reheat in the oven. Don't microwave your pizza, please.

Most leftovers taste great when repurposed either as nachos or pizza. Leftover butter chicken, in particular, is even better when topped with a layer of oozy melty cheese. You'll want to dice or shred the chicken for an optimal eating experience. And make sure to use cold leftover butter chicken for this recipe. The sauce thickens up a bit when cold, making it easier (and less messy) to spread on a pizza crust. The pickled jalapeños and mint are optional, but I like the way they cut through the richness of the butter chicken and cheese.

Preheat the oven to 450 degrees F. Place a rimmed baking sheet on the lower rack of the oven.

Pull the chicken pieces out of the butter chicken and dice or shred the meat (depending on your texture preference). Put the sauce and meat in separate bowls.

On a lightly floured work surface, use your hands to gently stretch out the dough. You want it to be 6 to 8 inches in diameter. Remove the baking sheet from the oven and drizzle it with olive oil, which will lightly sizzle, then place the stretched-out dough on the oiled pan. Bake for about 8 minutes, until the crust is mostly cooked through but still light in color.

Remove from the oven and top evenly with the butter chicken sauce, then the shredded mozzarella cheese, chicken pieces, red onion slices, and pickled jalapeños (if using). Return the pizza to the oven and bake until the cheese melts, another 3 minutes or so. Top with a flourish of cilantro and mint (if using). Once the pizza has somewhat cooled, slice and serve.

Naan Pizza

2 Simple Naan (page 255) or
    store-bought naan
¼ cup pesto
½ cup shredded mozzarella
¼ cup crumbled feta
8 to 10 kalamata or Castelvetrano
    olives, chopped
1 tablespoon capers, drained
4 marinated artichoke hearts,
    drained and chopped

❋ FREEZER NOTE

Cooked pizzas can be wrapped in alumi-num foil and frozen for up to 2 months. Reheat in the oven. Don't microwave your pizza, please.

I cannot think of a scenario in which naan pizza is not the answer. I only have 10 minutes to make something: make naan pizza. I have zero brain power to think of something to cook: make naan pizza. I want something delicious and easy: make naan pizza. I am feeding people with different food preferences and dietary restrictions: make naan pizza. They are extremely customizable and work with any pizza sauce/cheese/topping combination you can dream up.

I like to use leftover Simple Naan (page 255), but any store-bought version you like also works! (I am partial to the Stonefire brand.) So do flavored versions, like garlic naan. There is also no correct formula for toppings, so please use the recipe below as inspiration. I like pickly, salty ingredients on my pizza. But if tomato sauce with fresh mozzarella and basil is more your vibe? That works. Want to throw a fried egg and crumbled sausage on it and call it breakfast? Go for it. Naan is also a great base for any of the other pizza recipes in this chapter.

Preheat the oven to 375 degrees F. Line a rimmed baking sheet with aluminum foil or parchment paper.

Place the naan on the prepared baking sheet. Evenly spread each naan with half of the pesto, then top each with half of the shredded cheese. Distribute the crumbled feta, olives, capers, and artichoke hearts evenly on top. Bake for 7 to 9 minutes, until the cheese is melted and the naan is warmed through and slightly crispy on the bottom.

RICE & [

Comfort foods can take many forms, but rice and noodles are my pillars. Too many days without rice and my body and soul start to physically act out. And some days only a giant pile of pasta will solve whatever problem I am facing. You might not expect a set of noodle recipes in an Indian book, but the flavors work so well together, it should be standard.

NOODLES

Spinach Jeera Rice

1 cup white basmati rice

1½ cups baby spinach

1½ cups water, divided

2 tablespoons ghee or neutral oil

1½ teaspoons cumin seeds

1 inch cinnamon stick

1 bay leaf

2 whole cloves

2 green cardamom pods

1½ teaspoons salt, or to taste

1 teaspoon Kashmiri red chili powder

❄ **FREEZER NOTE**

This rice freezes well in an airtight container for a month or two. If reheating in the microwave, add a splash of water before cooking.

Jeera rice, which translates to cumin rice, is a staple of north Indian cooking. I got the idea to add pureed fresh spinach to the rice from Trader Joe's of all places. In its frozen aisle, the grocery store chain sells trays of paneer tikka masala with spinach rice. The verdant color of the rice really pops against the orange-red hue of the paneer tikka masala. It's worth noting that the spinach doesn't necessarily add a significant amount of flavor, but it's a fun riff on a classic dish. Also who doesn't love a secret vegetable? Turns out it's easy to make your own Paneer Tikka Masala (page 185) and spinach rice, and my recipe amps it up with spices like cloves, cardamom, and bay leaf. This rice is also delicious with a bowl of Chana Masala (page 197) or Rajma (page 191).

Rinse the rice, then let it soak in a bowl of water for 30 minutes. You can soak it for longer, but don't soak it for over 2 hours or it will become gummy. Drain.

In a blender, blend the spinach and ½ cup water; set aside.

Heat the ghee in a medium saucepan over medium heat until it shimmers. Add the cumin seeds and let them pop, then add the cinnamon, bay leaf, cloves, and cardamom pods and stir. Add the drained rice and sauté for 2 to 3 minutes, until the rice is fully coated and slightly dry. Pour in the spinach mixture, remaining 1 cup water, salt, and chili powder. Bring to a boil, cover, reduce to a simmer, and cook for 5 to 7 minutes, until the rice is tender. Turn off the heat, but keep the pan covered for about 10 minutes. Lift off the lid and fluff the rice with a fork before serving. If the rice feels too wet, let it cook for a few more minutes, uncovered, over medium heat.

Yogurt Rice

2 cups cooked medium-grain
    white rice, warm but not hot
½ cup plain full-fat yogurt
¼ cup whole milk (optional)
Salt to taste

TADKA
2 tablespoons neutral oil
2 teaspoons split urad dal
½ teaspoon mustard seeds
2 small dried red chiles
12 to 15 fresh curry leaves (optional)

◉ **SERVING NOTE**

I've had weeks where I have eaten yogurt rice for dinner three days in a row, usually with a bit of Cabbage Nu Shaak (page 223) mixed in, so I could say I ate a vegetable.

❄ **FREEZER NOTE**

Plain cooked white rice freezes well; let cool and freeze in an airtight container for up to 1 month. Thaw in the microwave to use. Do not freeze the yogurt rice.

Yogurt rice is known by many names in India and across its diaspora, including thayir sadam, dahi bhat, dahi chawal, mosaranna, and curd rice. For every name, there are even more variations. All of this is to say there is no single correct way to make yogurt rice. At its most stripped down, it is a bowl of cold plain yogurt mixed with warm-but-not-hot white rice and a bit of salt. If you need more flavor, you can add a spoonful of your favorite Indian pickle, or stir in grated carrots and pomegranate arils for crunch. The ultimate version, in my opinion, is made with a tadka, where mustard seeds, urad dal, and curry leaves are tempered in hot oil or ghee and drizzled generously on top of the bowl. I also prefer a non-Greek full-fat yogurt (full-fat dairy is where all the flavor is) and medium-grain rice, which tends to have a gentle stickiness that makes the dish even more comforting.

This is the best meal when you don't know what to feed yourself, or you are unable to muster up the energy to cook something that requires a knife and any chopping.

I hope this recipe can bring you as much comfort as it brings me.

Divide the rice between 2 bowls. Add half of the yogurt and milk (if using) to each and mix thoroughly.

Now make the tadka: In a small saucepan, heat the oil for about 2 minutes over medium heat, until the oil starts to shimmer. Add the urad dal and mustard seeds and let them sizzle for about 15 seconds. Turn off the heat, add the chiles and curry leaves (if using), and give it a good swirl. Pour the tadka evenly over the bowls of rice.

Vagharelo Bhaath

2 cups cooked white rice,
 cooled (ideally leftover)

1 cup plain full-fat yogurt (not Greek)

1 tablespoon neutral oil

½ teaspoon black mustard seeds

¼ teaspoon hing (asafoetida;
 optional but delicious)

¼ cup water

1 teaspoon salt

½ teaspoon ground turmeric

½ teaspoon Kashmiri red chili powder

❦ INGREDIENT NOTE

If you only have Greek yogurt, thin it out with a little bit of water or milk to make the consistency closer to regular full-fat yogurt.

🥣 STORAGE NOTE

You can use frozen white rice in this recipe, but I don't recommend freezing the cooked vagharelo bhaath. Any leftovers will keep well in an airtight container in the fridge for up to 2 days.

Practically every culture has a simple but genius use-up-leftover-rice recipe, and vagharelo bhaath is one of India's contributions to the canon. The dish hails from the western Indian state of Gujarat, where the name translates to rice (bhaath) that is cooked with tempered spices, which in Gujarati is called vaghar (aka tadka). Most Gujjus make this dish by stir-frying leftover white rice with sautéed onions, turmeric, and a tadka made from mustard seeds, green chiles, and, often, curry leaves. And then there is the way my family makes the dish. Say "vagharelo bhaath" in my parents' house, and you'll get a version cooked with yogurt. The result resembles a tangy, spicy Indian risotto. We have theories about why our family's version is so different, but this is how my grandmother made it, and how my mom continues to make it over 7,000 miles away from her childhood home. Her version, the version I share here, is the dish she makes me when I'm not feeling amazing (physically! emotionally!). Consider this recipe my version of Chicken Soup for the Soul. Hot Yogurty Rice for the Soul.

In a bowl, combine the rice and yogurt. Make sure every grain of rice is coated. Ideally you would cover the bowl and let the rice mixture sit overnight in the fridge or for a few hours at room temperature, but it isn't critical to the success of the recipe.

Heat the oil in a medium saucepan over medium heat. Add the mustard seeds and hing, if using. Let the mustard seeds sizzle for about 30 seconds and start popping. Add the rice mixture and reduce the heat to low. Stir in the water, salt, turmeric, and chili powder and turn the heat back up to medium. Cover the pan and let the rice cook undisturbed for 3 minutes. Take off the lid and give it a good stir to ensure nothing sticks to the bottom and burns. Re-cover the pan and let the rice cook for another 3 minutes. At this point it should have the texture of a loose risotto and there should be a little water left to cook off in the pan. Turn off the heat and let it sit covered for 5 minutes so that the mixture thickens to a lovely thick and creamy texture.

Biryani Baked in a Squash

PANEER

⅓ cup plain full-fat Greek yogurt

1 tablespoon garlic paste
   or 3 garlic cloves, minced

1½ teaspoons ginger paste
   or ½-inch piece fresh ginger grated

1 teaspoon Garam Masala (page 62)

1 teaspoon ground coriander

½ teaspoon ground cumin

½ teaspoon Kashmiri red chili powder

½ teaspoon salt

1 tablespoon chopped fresh cilantro

8 ounces paneer, cut into ½-inch cubes

CARAMELIZED ONIONS

3 tablespoons neutral oil or ghee

1 large white onion, thinly sliced

1 teaspoon salt

SAFFRON MILK

¼ cup whole milk

Pinch saffron threads

RICE

1 cup white basmati rice

2 cups water

1 teaspoon salt

3 green cardamom pods, smashed

3 to 4 whole cloves

1 large bay leaf

2-inch cinnamon stick

1 star anise pod

1 teaspoon neutral oil

Biryani is a special occasion dish for good reason: it's so much work. But don't let that scare you, as the payoff is worth it. Every. Single. Time. Good biryani is a visceral, tangible, and edible reminder that the human experience is mind-blowing. At its most basic, biryani is basmati rice, parboiled so that each grain cooks perfectly, layered with a generous amount of spices, vegetables, flavor elements like deeply caramelized onions, and typically a marinated protein.

One Thanksgiving, I got the idea to bake biryani inside a beautiful red kuri squash I found at the market. I love when serving vessels are edible (team bread bowls!), and visually it makes for a stunner of a main course, guaranteed to induce oohs and aahs.

I used paneer as the protein, though you could easily swap that for potatoes, hard-boiled eggs, chicken, or even turkey (especially at Thanksgiving). Just please do not skip the effort and time it takes to properly caramelize the onions—they are one of the main reasons biryani feels so extravagant. Serve this biryani with a giant bowl of Cucumber Raita (page 64) and don't forget that you can (and should) eat the squash.

First, marinate the paneer. In a medium bowl, combine the yogurt, garlic, ginger, garam masala, coriander, cumin, chili powder, salt, and cilantro. Add the paneer and toss to make sure each cube is well coated. Cover the bowl with a towel or plastic wrap and refrigerate for at least 1 hour.

Next up are the onions. Heat the oil in a large skillet over low heat. Add the onion and salt and let the onion caramelize, slowly, stirring every couple of minutes. The process will take 45 to 60 minutes before the onions are deep brown and fully caramelized. Remove the pan from the heat. (You can do this step the day before and refrigerate overnight in an airtight container.)

Recipe continues

SQUASH

1 large red kuri squash (should hold
    2 ½ to 3 cups packed filling)
1 tablespoon neutral oil or ghee
2 teaspoons Garam Masala (page 62)
1 teaspoon salt
½ bunch fresh cilantro leaves, chopped
½ bunch fresh mint leaves, chopped
Cucumber Raita (page 64), for serving

✤ INGREDIENT NOTE

You can use any edible squash that has a sturdy outside and can hold a lot of filling once hollowed out. I kept this recipe as simple as possible, but you could easily add more vegetables to the recipe, like fresh or frozen peas, cauliflower, or green beans. Just partially cook them and season with salt before layering with the paneer and rice.

✳ FREEZER NOTE

Cooked biryani, scraped out of the squash, can be frozen in an airtight container for up to 3 months and reheated in the microwave.

While the onions are cooking, in a small microwave-safe bowl, heat the milk in the microwave for a minute or so. Grind the saffron strands into a powder with either your fingers or a mortar and pestle, and swirl into the milk. The milk will take on a buttery yellow hue. Set aside.

Rinse the basmati rice at least twice until it runs clear, then put it in a large pot, cover with water, and let soak for at least 30 minutes, but ideally 1 hour. Drain the rice and return it to the pan. Add the 2 cups fresh water, salt, cardamom pods, cloves, bay leaf, cinnamon stick, star anise, and oil. Bring to a boil over medium heat and cook for 2 minutes. Drain the rice and whole spices and set aside.

Preheat the oven to 375 degrees F.

Cut the top off the squash and set the "lid" aside. Scrape out any seeds and accompanying goop (I like to use a grapefruit spoon for this). In a small bowl, mix the oil, garam masala, and salt to create a paste. Using a brush or your fingers, spread the seasoning mixture all over the inside of the squash.

Now it's time to layer the biryani. It is easiest to set the squash inside a large pot that fits in the oven. Pack one-third of the parboiled rice into the bottom of the squash, then splash with one-third of the saffron milk. Next distribute one-third of the caramelized onions over the rice, and one-third of the cilantro and mint. Then evenly pack in half of the marinated paneer. Follow with another one-third portion of the rice, saffron milk, onions, cilantro, and mint. Add the remaining paneer, then top with the remaining rice, saffron milk, onions, cilantro, and mint. Cover the squash with aluminum foil or the top of the squash and bake for 55 to 60 minutes, until the squash is cooked through. Let cool for about 15 minutes, then slice the squash top to bottom into quarters. Each quarter should show the layers of rice and paneer. I like to scrape the squash flesh into the biryani before eating. Serve with raita.

Mushroom Keema Pasta

1½ pounds mixed mushrooms

1 yellow onion, diced

4 tablespoons (½ stick) unsalted butter
   or neutral oil (butter tastes better)

1 tablespoon garlic paste
   or 3 garlic cloves, minced

1 tablespoon ginger paste *or*
   1–inch piece ginger, grated

½ green serrano pepper, minced

2 tablespoons tomato paste

1 tablespoon Garam Masala (page 62)

2 teaspoons Kashmiri red chili powder

2 teaspoons salt

1 teaspoon ground cumin

1 teaspoon ground coriander

½ teaspoon ground turmeric

¼ teaspoon ground cardamom

¼ teaspoon ground cinnamon

¼ cup milk (optional)

1 cup marinara sauce

1 tablespoon soy sauce

½ cup frozen green peas,
   thawed (optional)

8 ounces macaroni or other small
   pasta, cooked al dente according
   to package instructions

Fresh cilantro leaves, for garnish (optional)

❄ FREEZER NOTE

This freezes well with or without the pasta. Store in an airtight container in the freezer for up to 2 months. To reheat, pop into the microwave or plop into a pan on the stove (my preferred method).

Though I never grew up eating keema (often spelled qeema), I have friends who wax poetic about how their moms would toss leftover keema with tomato sauce and pasta to make a desi Bolognese. Never underestimate an auntie's ability to stretch leftovers.

Keema is traditionally made from heavily spiced and minced meat like lamb, beef, or chicken, but I opted to make a meatless version with mushrooms because I didn't want my vegetarians and vegans left behind and because I always have a pile of mushrooms in my fridge. If you aren't a mushroom person, you could very easily swap them out for soy crumbles or almost any minced animal protein of your choice.

The mushrooms must be minced before you proceed. You could absolutely do this with a knife and a lot of patience, or you could blitz the mushrooms in a food processor. (Be careful not to go too hard and turn the mushrooms into a paste; they should resemble little pebbles.) Transfer the mushrooms to a large bowl. Add the onion to the food processor and blitz (less tears!) to a fine dice. You don't want the onion pieces to be dramatically larger than the mushrooms.

In a large, heavy-bottomed pot, melt the butter over medium heat. Add the mushrooms and let them cook down and release their water, 3 to 4 minutes. Add the onion and cook until softened, 2 to 3 minutes. Add the garlic, ginger, and serrano pepper and let them mellow out, stirring the mixture, for a minute. Add the tomato paste, garam masala, chili powder, salt, cumin, coriander, turmeric, cardamom, and cinnamon and mix well. Cook for another 2 minutes, then add the milk if you are using it (it gives the keema a nice creamy edge). Stir and let cook for another minute or so. Congrats! You just made keema.

Mix in the marinara, soy sauce, and peas (if using) and cook until the tomato sauce is heated through. Toss with the cooked pasta and garnish with cilantro, if you like.

Makhani Mac and Cheese

MAKHANI SAUCE

2 tablespoons unsalted butter

½ white onion, minced

1 (5.3–ounce) tube or (6–ounce) can tomato paste

1 tablespoon garlic paste *or* 3 garlic cloves, minced

1½ teaspoons ginger paste *or* ½-inch piece ginger, grated

½ teaspoon salt

1 tablespoon Garam Masala (page 62)

1 teaspoon ground coriander

1 teaspoon ground cumin

BÉCHAMEL

2 tablespoons unsalted butter

2 tablespoons all-purpose flour

2 cups whole milk

1½ tablespoons kasoori methi (optional)

1 teaspoon sugar

Salt to taste

½ teaspoon ground black pepper

8 ounces Gouda cheese, shredded

8 ounces macaroni, shells, rotini, or other pasta of your choice, cooked al dente according to package instructions

❄ FREEZER NOTE

You can make the makhani sauce ahead of time and keep in an airtight container in the fridge for up to 5 days or in the freezer for up to 3 months. Leftover mac and cheese freezes incredibly well for up to 3 months. To reheat, warm it up either in the microwave or in a pan on the stove, straight from the freezer.

This recipe is inspired by the tikka masala mac that chef Preeti Mistry used to serve at her now-shuttered Oakland restaurant Navi Kitchen. She combined a riff on her butter chicken sauce with noodles, creating one of the best dishes on the menu. The idea of combining an Indian gravy with a from-scratch macaroni and cheese has stuck with me ever since, and so I started making this version, which blends a simplified makhani sauce, a creamy béchamel, and sauce-hugging noodles.

Too many macaroni and cheese recipes call for way too much expensive dairy. You could easily spend over $20 on the Gruyères and Fontinas of the world before you get the amount of cheese needed. That is why this recipe calls for a hunk of Gouda, which tends to be much more affordable.

If you prefer a baked mac and cheese, preheat the oven to 350 degrees F. Melt a little butter in a pan, add ½ cup panko bread crumbs, and toast until they are golden brown. Toss the toasted bread crumbs with a few handfuls of additional grated Gouda or parmesan and distribute evenly over the mac and cheese. Bake for 15 minutes or so, until the cheese is melted.

To make the makhani sauce, melt the butter in a Dutch oven or other large, heavy-bottomed pot over medium heat. Add the onion and cook until it starts to brown, 2 to 3 minutes. Add the tomato paste, garlic, ginger, and salt. Stir until the tomato paste starts to darken in color, 2 to 3 minutes. Add the garam masala, coriander, and cumin and stir until evenly combined. Remove the pan from the heat.

To make the béchamel, melt the butter in a large saucepan over medium heat. Add the flour and whisk until the roux smells toasty and takes on a light brown color, 1 to 2 minutes. Add the milk and makhani sauce and bring to a boil. Lower the heat and let the mixture simmer until it starts to thicken, 2 to 3 minutes. Add the kasoori methi (if using), sugar, salt, and pepper. Fold in the shredded Gouda. Add the noodles and stir well to make sure everything is combined.

Hakka Noodles

2 tablespoons neutral oil

1 tablespoon garlic paste
or 3 garlic cloves, minced

2 teaspoons ginger paste or ½-inch
piece fresh ginger, grated

½ white onion, thinly sliced

1 or 2 green serrano peppers, minced

4 scallions, chopped, greens
and whites separated

1 carrot, julienned

½ green bell pepper, julienned

½ red bell pepper julienned

½ cup shredded green cabbage (optional)

2 tablespoons soy sauce

2 teaspoons rice vinegar

2 teaspoons chili garlic sauce,
sambal oelek, or sriracha

1 teaspoon toasted sesame oil

½ teaspoon ground black pepper

½ teaspoon white pepper
(optional, but it's a vibe)

Salt to taste

1 (5.3-ounce) package hakka noodles
(see Ingredient Note), cooked
according to package instructions

❧ INGREDIENT NOTE

You can find hakka noodles at any Indian grocery store. I like a brand called Ching's. If you can't find them, you can use spaghetti or another thin wheat noodle.

❄ FREEZER NOTE

You can freeze the cooked noodles in an airtight container for up to 2 months.

As a teenager, whenever I would go to India, my cousin and I would sneak out to our favorite Indo-Chinese roadside stall to eat plates of these noodles. Even though my mouth was on fire and my eyes were watering, I could not stop eating them. I wish everyone could eat Hakka noodles served hot on the side of the street, but this recipe is the next best thing.

You can customize the hakka noodles as you wish: add more vegetables for more crunch and texture (or nutrients), or double or triple the chile if you like the dragon-breathing-fire level of hot. This dish comes together quickly and can feed a crowd. Serve with Cauliflower Manchurian (page 240) and Chili Paneer Dumplings (page 213) for a full feast.

Heat the neutral oil in a large skillet over medium heat. Add the garlic and ginger and fry for 30 seconds. Add the onion, serrano peppers, and scallion whites and cook for 2 minutes, until the onion starts to turn translucent. Add the carrot, bell peppers, and cabbage (if using) and cook for another 3 to 4 minutes, until the vegetables have started to soften.

In a small bowl, whisk together the soy sauce, rice vinegar, chili garlic sauce, sesame oil, black pepper, white pepper (if using), and salt.

Add the noodles to the pan with the cooked vegetables, then pour over the sauce and mix until everything is evenly coated. Remove the pan from the heat and garnish with the scallion greens.

Maggi Ramen Bowl

1 large egg

2 teaspoons neutral oil, divided

4 ounces king oyster, shiitake, or other fresh mushrooms of choice

1 tablespoon ginger paste *or* 1-inch piece fresh ginger, grated

1 tablespoon garlic paste *or* 3 garlic cloves, minced

2 scallions, chopped, greens and whites separated

1½ tablespoons soy sauce

2 teaspoons chili garlic sauce or sambal oelek (optional)

1 teaspoon toasted sesame oil

3 cups broth or water

2 (2.46-ounce) packages Maggi Masala 2-Minute Noodles, seasoning packets reserved

⅓ cup frozen corn kernels, thawed

1 cup baby spinach, wilted

1 slice American cheese (optional)

¼ teaspoon white sesame seeds

◉ **SERVING NOTE**

I like to melt a slice of American cheese—my favorite instant noodle topping—on the ramen, too.

❄ **FREEZER NOTE**

This does not freeze well.

Maggi noodles are always described as Indian ramen. While they are India's answer to instant noodles, the real question is, can you transform Maggi into a bowl of ramen? You know the kind with bouncy noodles, a boisterous broth, and an assortment of fun toppings? Turns out you can—sort of.

I deeply admire and respect the art of Japanese ramen making, but this recipe does not feature a tare, dashi, kombu, or a stock that has been simmering for three days straight. What it does have is a zippy, deeply savory base, lots of curly noodles, and a slate of toppings, including a jammy soft-boiled egg. It's as fun to eat as a proper bowl of ramen but comes together in only 20 minutes.

First, make a soft-boiled egg for your ramen. Heat 1 inch of water in a small saucepan. Add the egg, cover the pan, and let the egg cook for 6 minutes. Transfer the egg to a bowl filled with ice water.

Heat 1 teaspoon neutral oil in a large skillet over high heat. Add the mushrooms and sauté until the water has cooked out of the mushrooms and they are tender and golden brown, 2 to 5 minutes. Using a slotted spoon, transfer the mushrooms to a bowl. Add the remaining 1 teaspoon neutral oil to the pan. When it is hot, add the ginger, garlic, and scallion whites and sauté for 30 seconds. Add the soy sauce, chili garlic sauce (if you like a little heat!), sesame oil, broth, and both Maggi seasoning packets and bring to a boil. Add both packages of dried noodles and boil for 2 to 3 minutes, until the noodles are cooked through but still have a bit of bite.

Pour the noodles and broth into a bowl. Peel the soft-boiled egg, cut it in half, and place the halves in the bowl. Place the corn kernels in one section of the bowl, the spinach in another. Slide on a piece of cheese, if using, and create a pile of scallion greens to mound in the center of the bowl. Sprinkle on the sesame seeds and serve.

Lemon Seviyan

2 tablespoons neutral oil

1 teaspoon cumin seeds

1 tablespoon urad dal

20 fresh or dried curry leaves
  (see Ingredient Note)

¼ cup unsalted peanuts or cashews

½ green serrano pepper, minced

1 cup wheat vermicelli noodles

1 cup water

1 teaspoon salt

½ teaspoon ground turmeric

½ teaspoon Kashmiri red chili powder

Juice of 1 small lemon

2 tablespoons chopped fresh
  cilantro (optional)

🌿 INGREDIENT NOTE

If you cannot find fresh curry leaves, you can use dried curry leaves after soaking them in water for 10 minutes to rehydrate them. You can also find wheat vermicelli noodles labeled as fideo noodles in many grocery stores.

🥣 STORAGE NOTE

Seviyan does not freeze well, but it keeps great in an airtight container in the fridge for up to 3 days.

When most people think of Indian food, they don't exactly think of noodles. While rice and flatbreads tend to be the dominant carbohydrates, Indians are fond of one noodle type in particular: vermicelli. The thin noodles cook quickly and absorb flavor well. Lemon seviyan is one of my favorite ways to eat vermicelli; it's also called lemon semiya, semiya upma, or vermicelli upma, depending on where you are. The crunchy urad dal, crispy curry leaves, and lemon juice combine with the noodles to create a dish that tastes fresh and feels light. It's one of my go-to quick lunches, especially on a weekday, and I like to pair it with some sliced cucumber or a piece of fruit.

Heat the oil in a medium saucepan over medium-high heat until glistening. Add the cumin seeds and let them pop. Turn the heat down to medium, add the urad dal, and cook until toasted, about 2 minutes. Add the curry leaves, nuts, and serrano pepper and stir for a minute until the nuts are toasted. Add the noodles and stir until they are evenly coated with the oil mixture and slightly toasted, about 2 minutes. Add the water, salt, turmeric, and chili powder and stir to combine. Turn up the heat and bring the mixture to a boil. Turn the heat back down, cover, and let simmer for 3 minutes, or until most of the water is absorbed. Stir in the lemon juice, cover, and let simmer for another 1 to 2 minutes, until all the liquid is fully absorbed and the noodles are tender. Turn off the heat and let it sit, covered, for 5 to 7 minutes. Sprinkle with the cilantro (if using) and divide between 2 bowls.

Saag Paneer Lasagna
(aka LaSAAGna)

BÉCHAMEL

8 tablespoons (2 sticks) unsalted butter

½ cup all-purpose flour

1 quart whole milk, at room temperature

½ teaspoon ground black pepper

¼ teaspoon ground nutmeg

½ cup grated parmesan

LASAGNA

1 (12-ounce) block paneer, shredded

24 sheets no-boil lasagna noodles

1 recipe Saag Paneer (page 215)
   made *without* the paneer

¼ cup grated parmesan

❄ FREEZER NOTE

Once the lasagna has cooled to room temperature, freeze individual portions in airtight containers for up to 3 months. The lasagna reheats well in a microwave or an oven.

I have a lot of very strong opinions when it comes to lasagna. The biggest one? People put too many things in lasagna! It doesn't need the fistfuls of mozzarella, heavy globs of ricotta, vegetables that are too chunky, and ladles of marinara sauce that are often too watery. The optimal lasagna is made from lots of neat, thin layers of pasta, vegetables, and sauce, with minimal cheese. Lasagna should feel indulgent, but not like it is going to murder your digestive system.

I am extremely partial to spinach lasagna with a cheesy béchamel sauce. I love the contrast of the bright green layers against the beige pasta, and the way the béchamel makes the dish rich and creamy but not too heavy. One day as I was making Saag Paneer (page 215), it dawned on me that it would make for the perfect lasagna filling, with the cilantro and spices giving it a little more depth and oomph than a standard spinach lasagna filling. To make this version, I use the saag paneer base but keep the paneer to the side so I can crumble it before gently pan-frying, so that you get a little salty paneer in each bite.

As the kids say these days, this lasagna fully slaps. It's a hit every time I make it, with high demand for any leftovers. It also freezes incredibly well, making it a good option to gift new parents or for meal prep. This lasagna is now a staple of my Thanksgiving table (along with the Biryani Baked in a Squash on page 159) and I hope it finds a way onto your table, too.

Recipe continues

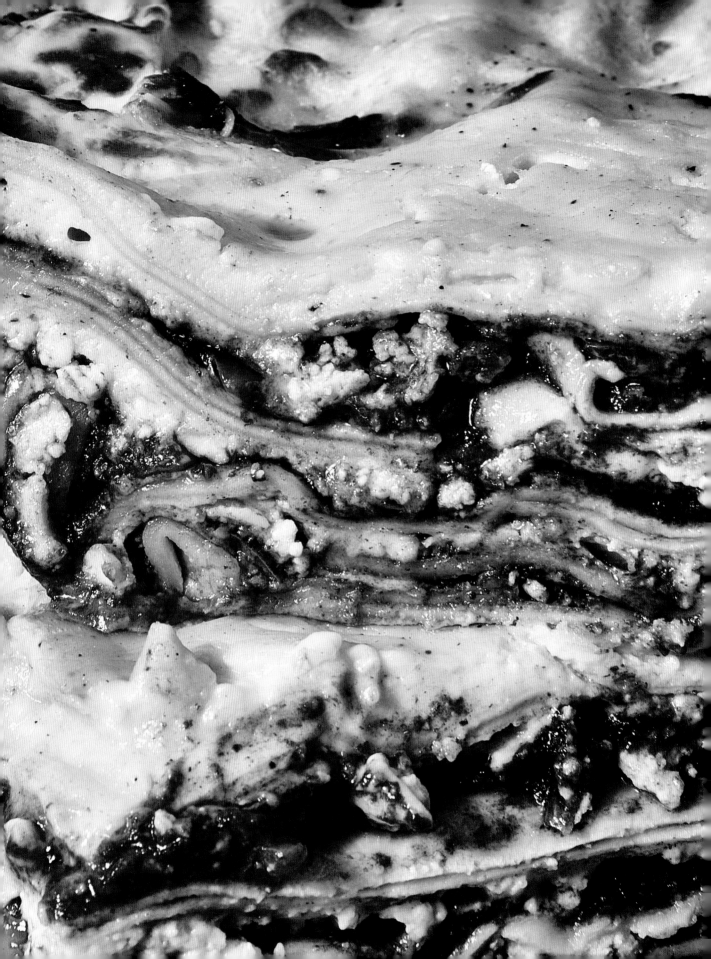

Preheat the oven to 400 degrees F. Oil a 9 x 13–inch baking dish with tall sides.

To make the béchamel, melt the butter in a large pot over low heat. Add the flour and whisk until the roux turns golden, 3 to 4 minutes. Add the milk, turn the heat up to medium, and continuously stir the mixture until it starts to bubble and thicken. It should coat the back of a wooden spoon when ready, 4 to 5 minutes. Remove from the heat and fold in the black pepper, nutmeg, and parmesan, whisking until smooth. Set aside.

To make the lasagna, spread a thin layer of béchamel on the bottom of the prepared baking dish, then add 6 sheets of noodles, breaking the noodles as you need to fit the pan. Next spread one-third of the saag sauce over the noodles, then one-third of the paneer shreds, and one-quarter of the remaining béchamel. Repeat this process 2 more times, starting with another layer of noodles. Finish with a final layer of 6 noodles, the remaining béchamel, and then the parmesan. Here's how it will look:

Cover the lasagna with aluminum foil and bake for 35 minutes. Remove the foil and bake for about 15 minutes, until the lasagna is cooked through and lightly golden on top. Let the lasagna cool for at least 15 minutes before slicing and serving.

Lasagna Layering Guide

TOP LAYER: NOODLES, BÉCHAMEL, PARM

MIDDLE LAYER 1: NOODLES, SAAG SAUCE, PANEER CRUMBLES, BÉCHAMEL

MIDDLE LAYER 2: NOODLES, SAAG SAUCE, PANEER CRUMBLES, BÉCHAMEL

BOTTOM LAYER: THIN LAYER OF BÉCHAMEL, NOODLES, SAAG SAUCE, PANEER CRUMBLES, BÉCHAMEL

Indian meals are rarely centered around a singular piece of protein, like a roast chicken or a pork chop, then filled out with a handful of sides like buttered noodles or steamed green beans. Instead, they are usually a collection of dishes, an exercise in mixing and matching. These dishes are often consumed together—but there are plenty of recipes in this chapter that are great by themselves, or with a scoop of hot white rice.

BIG PLATES

BIG BOWLS

Rajma Nachos

1 (16–ounce) bag corn tortilla chips

1½ cups Rajma (page 191)

1 pound cheddar cheese, shredded

½ small white onion, diced

12 to 15 pickled jalapeño slices

½ avocado, diced

⅓ cup plain full-fat yogurt

2 teaspoons water

½ teaspoon Chaat Masala (page 63)

⅓ cup Tamarind Chutney (page 52)

⅓ cup Cilantro-Mint Chutney (page 50)

❋ FREEZER NOTE

Do not freeze.

I often make rajma simply to make rajma nachos. The stewy, almost jammy kidney beans make for a spectacular nacho base, especially when you need to switch it up from the usual rotation of black beans or ground beef. The toppings on these nachos are pretty standard—lots of cheddar cheese (please shred your own rather than buy the pre-shredded stuff!), diced onion, avocado, and pickled jalapeños—plus two types of chutney and a chaat masala–spiked yogurt sauce (they are Indian nachos after all).

I make this pretty regularly as a treat-yourself weeknight dinner, or whenever I have a bunch of friends coming over. It comes together quickly if you have the rajma already on hand. The nachos also work really well with leftover Dal Makhani (page 209) instead of rajma and as part of a game day spread with Tandoori Chicken Wings (page 86) and a platter of Masala Poutine (page 78).

Preheat the oven to 375 degrees F. Line a large rimmed baking sheet with parchment paper or aluminum foil.

Spread the chips in an even layer across the prepared baking sheet so that there are no gaps between the chips. Using a spoon, dollop the rajma evenly over the chips, then sprinkle the cheese over everything. Bake for 6 to 8 minutes, until the cheese is fully melted and gooey.

Scatter the onion evenly across the nachos, then the pickled jalapeños and avocado.

In a small bowl, mix the yogurt, water, and chaat masala (it should be pretty runny). Drizzle the yogurt mixture over the nachos, followed by both chutneys. Eat immediately.

Aloo Paratha Quesadillas

QUICK RAITA

½ cup plain full-fat yogurt

1 teaspoon Chaat Masala (see page 63)

½ teaspoon salt

QUESADILLAS

8 Super Flaky Parathas (page 247)
    or store-bought frozen parathas
    (see Ingredient Note on page 29)

1 tablespoon neutral oil, plus
    more for cooking

1 teaspoon cumin seeds

1 green serrano pepper, minced

½ white onion, diced

1½ teaspoons ginger paste *or*
    ½-inch piece fresh ginger, grated

1½ teaspoons salt

4 small red potatoes, boiled and peeled

1 tablespoon amchur

1 tablespoon Garam Masala (page 62)

1 teaspoon ground coriander

½ teaspoon Kashmiri red chili powder

¼ cup roughly chopped fresh cilantro

4 ounces cheddar cheese, grated

Spicy Cilantro Chutney
    (page 51), for serving

Indians are savants when it comes to combining multiple carbohydrates into one dish, and aloo parathas, or flatbreads lovingly stuffed with spiced potatoes, are a premier example. Not much in this world can rival the joy of a piping-hot aloo paratha with a bowl of cold raita and some freshly cut fruit. The craving hits more than I care to admit, but I often do not have the time (or, more accurately, the patience) to make parathas from scratch, so I started making these quesadillas instead—the lazy person's aloo paratha. You'll use the same components—soft parathas and spiced potato filling—upgraded with a bit of cheddar and in a much speedier format. I like these for breakfast, but they also work as a quick lunch or even a midnight snack.

To make the raita, in a small bowl, combine the yogurt, chaat masala, and salt. Mix until well combined and set aside.

If using frozen parathas, heat them according to the package instructions.

In a medium skillet, heat the oil over medium-high heat. Add the cumin seeds and let them sizzle for 10 seconds (watch closely because they can burn quickly). Add the serrano pepper and stir-fry for 10 seconds. Add the onion, ginger, and salt and cook, stirring frequently, for 4 to 5 minutes, until the onion has softened and turned golden. Remove the pan from the heat.

In a medium bowl, lightly mash the potatoes (they should be chunky!). Add the amchur, garam masala, coriander, chili powder, and cilantro and give it a rough mix. Add the cooked onion mixture and combine well.

Recipe continues

Spoon an equal amount of the potato mixture on one half of each paratha, top with about 2 tablespoons cheddar, and fold over the other half of the paratha. You should have a cute half-moon shape.

Heat 1 teaspoon oil in a medium skillet over medium heat. Place a quesadilla in the pan and cook for 2 minutes on each side, or until the outside is browned and the cheese is gooey. Repeat to cook the remaining quesadillas, adding more oil as necessary. Cut the quesadillas into halves and serve with the raita and chutney.

Zucchini Mutiya

4 medium zucchini, grated
    and squeezed dry

2 cups baby spinach, roughly chopped

1½ tablespoons sugar

Juice of 1 lemon

1 cup semolina or Cream of Wheat

¾ cup whole wheat flour (atta)

¾ cup besan or chickpea flour

½ cup cooked white rice

2 tablespoons neutral oil

1 tablespoon salt

1 tablespoon Kashmiri red chili powder

2 teaspoons ground turmeric

TADKA

¼ cup neutral oil

2 teaspoons black mustard seeds

2 tablespoons white sesame seeds

Pinch hing (asafoetida; optional)

Juice of ½ lemon

1 teaspoon salt

Ketchup and/or Spicy Cilantro
    Chutney (page 51), for serving

🌿 INGREDIENT NOTE

If you are struggling to find semolina, you can easily purchase it at your local Indian grocery store under the name "sooji," but Cream of Wheat works as well. You can also use any leftover cooked rice you have on hand, including Khichdi (page 206). The rice helps bind the mutiya together.

Every summer, hundreds of thousands of people across the US face the same issue: What the hell should they do with all this homegrown zucchini their neighbor gifted them? More times than not, the answer is "make zucchini bread," but I'm here to offer you an alternative: zucchini mutiya. They're a savory, steamed dumpling (of sorts) made with semolina and besan or chickpea flour, and they use up several cups of shredded squash, no oven required. Instead, you steam and then pan-fry them with a tadka for maximum crispy edges and a second round of seasoning. This is a very versatile base recipe that can be used to make mutiya with almost any other vegetable, if you maintain a 2-to-1 ratio of vegetables to flour. I'll often sub out the zucchini for dudi, or bottle gourd. I eat mutiya with ketchup, but they also pair well with Spicy Cilantro Chutney (page 51).

In a large bowl, combine the zucchini, spinach, sugar, and lemon juice.

In another large bowl, combine the semolina, whole wheat flour, besan flour, rice, oil, salt, chili powder, and turmeric and stir until well mixed.

Add the flour mixture to the zucchini in batches, mixing until a soft but not sticky dough forms. If the dough feels too wet, add more semolina. Wet your hands and shape the mutiya dough into 10 to 12 logs that are about 2 inches thick and 8 inches long.

Pour an inch or two of water into a large pot and add a steamer basket. Bring the water to a boil. Working in batches as necessary, place the dough logs in the steamer, cover, and let them cook for 16 to 17 minutes, until the dough is cooked all the way through and the logs have a slightly springy texture. It's normal for the logs to expand and touch each other.

Recipe continues

Mutiya freezes well in an airtight container for at least 3 months. Simply thaw at
room temperature and then microwave or
reheat on the stovetop.

Slice the logs into ½-inch-thick pieces. You can eat these immediately, but I prefer them crisped up and tossed with a tadka.
To make the tadka, heat the oil in a large nonstick skillet over
medium-high heat. Add the mustard seeds and let them pop.
Turn the heat down to low, lift the pan slightly off the heat, add
the sesame seeds, and swirl them in the oil. Add the hing, if
using. Place the pan back on the flame and add the cut mutiya
pieces. In a small bowl, combine the lemon juice and salt and
mix well. Drizzle over the mutiya and give everything a good
stir. Turn the heat up to medium and let the mutiya crisp up,
stirring occasionally, for 5 to 7 minutes. Serve with ketchup
and/or chutney.

Lemon Rasam

1 cup toor dal, rinsed and drained

5 cups water, divided

1 tablespoon ghee

2 medium tomatoes, diced

2 green serrano peppers, minced

1½ tablespoons ginger paste *or*
   1½-inch piece fresh ginger, grated

1 tablespoon garlic paste
   or 3 garlic cloves, minced

½ teaspoon salt

¼ teaspoon ground turmeric

TADKA

2 tablespoons ghee

1 teaspoon black mustard seeds

½ teaspoon cumin seeds

⅛ teaspoon hing (asafoetida; optional)

15 to 20 fresh curry leaves

2 tablespoons chopped fresh cilantro

Juice of 1 lemon

❄ FREEZER NOTE

You can freeze rasam in an airtight container for up to 3 months. Thaw in the fridge before reheating. Make a little more tadka and mix it in before eating.

The human body is said to be at least 60 percent water. I am pretty sure most south Indians would agree that their bodies are more like 30 percent water, 30 percent rasam. Rasam is life. It's easy to see why: rasam is brothier than most north Indian dals, extremely comforting, and comes in several varieties. The most popular version is made with tamarind, but I am partial to this one flavored with garlic and lots of lemon juice. This recipe is from Rekha Auntie, who not only makes incredible rasam but is also the mom of one of my closest friends, Mahima. The rasam is meant to be thin, only slightly thicker than chicken soup, so add more water if needed. While rasam is delicious on its own, I like it best ladled over a mound of white rice.

Combine the toor dal and 3 cups water in an Instant Pot and cook on high pressure for 10 minutes. Once it is cooked, mix well with a spatula or whisk to break up the lentils.

In a large, heavy-bottomed pot, melt the ghee over medium heat. Add the tomatoes and cook until soft, 2 to 3 minutes. Stir in the serrano peppers, ginger, garlic, salt, and turmeric and cook for 1 minute. Add the remaining 2 cups water and bring to a boil. Turn the heat down to a simmer and let cook for 10 minutes. Add the cooked toor dal and let the rasam simmer for another 5 minutes. If it feels thick, add additional water. The texture should be quite soupy, almost as thin as a broth. Remove the pan from the heat.

To make the tadka, in a small saucepan, melt the ghee over medium heat. Add the mustard seeds and let them pop. Add the cumin seeds, hing (if using), and curry leaves and remove the pan from the heat. Add the cilantro and lemon juice and give it a swirl. Pour the tadka over the rasam in the larger pot and stir to combine. Serve hot.

Paneer Tikka Masala

3 tablespoons ghee or neutral oil, divided

2 large tomatoes, roughly chopped (see Ingredient Note)

1 large white onion, roughly chopped

3 cups whole milk

1 bay leaf

2 whole cloves

3 green cardamom pods

1-inch cinnamon stick

1 tablespoon Garam Masala (page 62)

2 teaspoons Kashmiri red chili powder

1 teaspoon ground cumin

½ teaspoon ground turmeric

½ cup water

2 tablespoons chopped cashews (optional)

2 tablespoons sugar

1½ teaspoons salt, or to taste

1 pound paneer, cut into ½-inch cubes

¼ cup kasoori methi

1 to 2 tablespoons heavy cream (optional)

Spinach Jeera Rice, for serving (page 152)

🌿 INGREDIENT NOTE

If you don't want to make your own shahi paneer masala blend, you can easily find a premade version at any Indian store, such as MDH or Everest brand—just use 2 or 3 tablespoons instead of the garam masala, Kashmiri red chili powder, cumin, and turmeric.

❄ FREEZER NOTE

PTM freezes exceptionally well in an airtight container for at least 6 months. Thaw in the fridge or on the counter before heating up and serving.

I think I could eat paneer tikka masala, or PTM, every single day—if it's made properly. In theory it's an incredibly simple dish: cubes of paneer bobbing in a creamy tomato gravy. But restaurants often depend on huge glugs of heavy cream to achieve a gravy with the proper silky texture. This not only makes the dish too rich, but it also mutes the spices that make paneer tikka masala so good in the first place. Restaurants also tend to chuck in huge pieces of paneer, which means you don't get a little bit of paneer in each bite. With a little bit of patience—and milk—it is possible to create a luxurious tomato-onion gravy with no heavy cream. If your tomatoes are out of season, add a couple of tablespoons of tomato paste to boost the flavor. If using canned tomatoes, look for a 15-ounce can of crushed tomatoes. Don't skip out on adding the kasoori methi, or dried fenugreek, at the end. It is what separates good PTM from great PTM.

Heat 2 tablespoons ghee in a large pot or Dutch oven over medium heat. Add the tomatoes and onion and sauté until the fat starts to separate and the tomatoes and onion are jammy, about 10 minutes. Transfer the cooked-down tomato-onion mixture to a blender, add the milk, and blend until smooth.

Wipe out the pot, then heat the remaining 1 tablespoon ghee over medium heat. Add the bay leaf, cloves, cardamom pods, cinnamon stick, and tomato-milk mixture. Stir in the garam masala, chili powder, cumin, turmeric, water, and cashews (if using). Turn the heat up to high and bring the gravy to a boil. Turn the heat down to low and simmer, stirring occasionally, until the gravy thickens, 5 to 7 minutes. Add the sugar and salt and stir, then add the paneer cubes and kasoori methi. Let the paneer tikka masala simmer for 5 minutes, then turn off the heat. Drizzle in the cream if you prefer a richer gravy. Serve with a side of spinach jeera rice for a simple, quick meal.

Shrimp Moilee

1 tablespoon coconut oil or neutral oil

2 tablespoons garlic paste *or*
   6 garlic cloves, minced

1 tablespoon ginger paste *or* 1-inch
   piece fresh ginger, grated

2 or 3 green serrano peppers, seeded
   (unless you love heat!) and minced

10 fresh curry leaves, chopped

1 white onion, diced

1½ teaspoons ground turmeric

1 teaspoon salt

½ teaspoon ground black pepper

2 teaspoons lemon juice

1 (13.5-ounce) can full-fat coconut milk

1 teaspoon sugar

24 large shrimp, peeled and deveined

Fresh cilantro leaves, for garnish (optional)

❄ FREEZER NOTE

The base sauce (without the shrimp) will
stay well in an airtight container in the
freezer for at least 3 months. Thaw it in the
fridge or on the counter and then reheat
on the stovetop, with any proteins or vegetables you like.

🍴 EXTRA CREDIT

Try it with sweet potatoes or even tofu, too.

It's worth always keeping a can of coconut milk in your pantry simply to be able to make moilee whenever the craving strikes. I know butter chicken gets all the love when it comes to saucy Indian dishes, but moilee is the overlooked and underestimated kid in high school that grows up to be very cool, good-looking, and rich. The south Indian dish is made with a whole can of coconut milk, giving it a lush, velvety texture. The sauce itself is a gorgeous pastel yellow that should absolutely be a crayon color.

Moilee is the best base for seafood; I make moilee with shrimp, as in this recipe, though you will often find it on menus as meen moilee, "meen" meaning fish. Moilee comes together quickly, with minimal chopping, so it's an ideal din-ner for busy nights, especially when served with a side of white rice.

Heat the oil in a large skillet over high heat. Add the garlic, ginger, serrano peppers, and curry leaves and cook, stirring constantly, until the curry leaves start to crackle, 1 to 2 minutes. Add the onion, turn the heat down to medium, and cook, stirring occasionally, until the onion softens and becomes translucent, about 5 minutes. Add the turmeric, salt, black pepper, and lemon juice and stir until well combined. Pour in the coconut milk and let it cook for 2 minutes. Stir in the sugar. Add the shrimp and simmer for 5 minutes or so, until the shrimp are cooked through. Garnish with cilantro, if you like.

Classic Butter Chicken

MARINADE

½ cup plain full-fat Greek yogurt

1½ tablespoons garlic paste
   or 5 garlic cloves, minced

1½ tablespoons ginger paste or
   1½-inch piece fresh ginger, grated

1 tablespoon Garam Masala (page 62)

1 teaspoon Kashmiri red chili powder

1 teaspoon salt

2 pounds boneless, skinless chicken
   thighs or breasts, cut into 1-inch cubes

MAKHANI SAUCE

3 tablespoons unsalted butter

1 tablespoon neutral oil

1 tablespoon Kashmiri red chili powder

2 teaspoons Garam Masala (page 62)

1 teaspoon ground cumin

1 tablespoon garlic paste
   or 3 garlic cloves, minced

1 tablespoon ginger paste or 1-inch
   piece fresh ginger, grated

1 green serrano pepper, minced

1 (5.3-ounce) tube or (6-ounce)
   can tomato paste

1 cup half-and-half

1½ teaspoons sugar

¼ teaspoon ground cardamom

Salt to taste

TO FINISH

1 tablespoon cold butter

1½ teaspoons kasoori methi (optional)

I almost didn't include a recipe for butter chicken (aka murgh makhani) in this book. Indian cooking is so diverse and expansive and exciting that it can be frustrating when people seem to only know this one dish. But, while there is so much more to Indian food than murgh makhani, it's the most popular Indian dish in America for good reason: it is incredibly delicious. A creamy, spiced sauce, tender meat—what is not to love?

The most important step in making butter chicken, and the one you cannot skip, is to marinate the protein in a spiced yogurt mixture before cooking. This helps keep the meat tender and adds another layer of flavor beyond the sauce. I kept this recipe mild, but if you like things spicier, double the amount of Kashmiri red chili powder or serrano pepper. I also often swap out the chicken for tofu or paneer for a stellar vegetarian version. Be sure to still marinate the tofu or paneer, as you would the chicken. Serve with plenty of Simple Parathas (page 244), Simple Naan (page 255), or white rice.

In a medium bowl, combine the yogurt, garlic, ginger, garam masala, chili powder, and salt and mix until smooth. Add the chicken pieces and toss until the chicken is completely coated. Cover and refrigerate for at least 1 hour, or preferably overnight for maximum flavor.

Preheat the oven to 400 degrees F. Line a rimmed baking sheet or roasting pan with parchment paper (or use a nonstick sheet or pan).

Spread out the marinated chicken pieces on the prepared
baking sheet or roasting pan and bake for 20 to 25 minutes,
until the chicken is cooked all the way through but still juicy. (It
should hit an internal temp of 164 degrees F.) Move the baking
sheet up to the top rack, turn the oven to broil, and broil for
2 minutes so that the chicken develops a gentle smoky flavor.
Remove from the oven and let it cool.

To make the makhani sauce, in a large, heavy-bottomed skillet,
melt the butter over medium heat—it is butter chicken, after all.
Add the oil, chili powder, garam masala, cumin, garlic, ginger,
and serrano pepper and stir for 20 to 30 seconds, until fragrant.
Add the tomato paste and let it caramelize, stirring constantly,
about 5 minutes. Stir in the half-and-half, sugar, cardamom, and
salt, then add the chicken and bring the sauce to a boil until it is
slightly thickened, 2 to 3 minutes. Turn the heat down to low and
stir in the cold butter and kasoori methi, if using.

Rajma

1 cup dried kidney beans *or* 2 (15-ounce) cans kidney beans, drained and rinsed

Water, as needed

2 tablespoons neutral oil

½ medium white onion, minced

2 medium Roma tomatoes, diced, or ½ cup canned crushed tomatoes

1 tablespoon Garam Masala (page 62)

2 teaspoons ground coriander

1 teaspoon ground cumin

½ teaspoon ground turmeric

½ teaspoon Kashmiri red chili powder

1 or 2 green cardamom pods

1-inch cinnamon stick

1 bay leaf

Salt to taste

❄ FREEZER NOTE

Rajma freezes exceptionally well. Store in an airtight container for at least 3 months and reheat on the stove to make it feel as fresh as possible.

🍴 EXTRA CREDIT

Leftover rajma serves as an incredible base for Indian-inspired nachos (see page 174).

A staple of Punjabi cooking, a pot of rajma transforms kidney beans into the most luxurious ingredient. While a lot of restaurants rely on heavy cream to achieve that effect, it's completely unnecessary. The real trick is patience. You must let the beans simmer properly until they become velvety and tender, and there is no way to rush that process. Kidney beans prepared from the dried bean versus from a can also tend to be creamier, but canned beans will still be delicious in this recipe. One of my favorite meals is a bowl of rajma with a small stack of Simple Parathas (page 244) and a small bowl of lightly sweetened yogurt with a pinch of cardamom; rajma is also good with rice.

If using dried beans, rinse them 3 times under cold running water, put them in a slow cooker, add 2½ cups water, cover, and cook on high for 6 to 7 hours, until the beans are tender and soft. Drain.

Heat the oil in a large pot over medium-high heat. Add the onion and cook for 3 minutes, until it just starts to take on color. Add the tomatoes and turn the heat down to medium. Cook, stirring occasionally, until the oil starts to separate out from the mixture and the tomatoes start to look a little jammy, about 10 minutes. Add the garam masala, coriander, cumin, turmeric, chili powder, cardamom pods, cinnamon stick, and bay leaf and stir to evenly combine. Add the beans and 1 cup water if you started with dried beans or 3 cups water if you're using canned beans, then season with salt. Bring to a boil, then turn the heat down to a simmer, cover, and cook until the beans are supremely tender, at least 5 minutes for dried beans or at least 15 minutes for canned beans. The rajma should be quite saucy but not watery; keep simmering with the lid off if the beans are too watery. Keep in mind that the sauce thickens as it cools.

Punjabi Egg Curry

2 tablespoons neutral oil

1 medium white onion, minced

1 green serrano pepper, minced

1½ teaspoons garlic paste
   or 2 garlic cloves, minced

1½ teaspoons ginger paste or
   1-inch piece ginger, grated

1 bay leaf

2-inch cinnamon stick (optional)

2 teaspoons Garam Masala (page 62)

1 teaspoon salt

1 teaspoon Kashmiri red chili powder

1 teaspoon ground turmeric

½ teaspoon ground coriander

4 Roma tomatoes, pureed, or
   1 (14.5-ounce) can crushed tomatoes

1 tablespoon kasoori methi (optional)

1 cup water

8 large eggs, hard-boiled (see
   Ingredient Note on page 73),
   peeled, and halved lengthwise

1 tablespoon minced fresh cilantro,
   for garnish (optional)

❄ **FREEZER NOTE**

The gravy, minus the eggs, freezes incredibly well. To do this, cook the recipe as written until it is time to add the hard-boiled eggs. Let the gravy base cool, then divide into airtight containers that serve one or two people. Freeze for at least 2 months.

Of all the egg formats that exist—silky-smooth scrambled eggs, yolky poached eggs, a good crispy fried egg, and so on—the hard-boiled egg doesn't get enough respect. In this recipe, it's the star. Egg curries exist with all sorts of exciting regional variations across India, but one of the most popular is from the northern state of Punjab. This egg curry features hard-boiled eggs simmered in a thick tomato-onion sauce that is well spiced but not overly spicy. It's delicious over rice, but even better with Simple Parathas (page 244).

Heat the oil in a medium skillet over low heat. Add the onion and cook until golden, 4 to 5 minutes. Add the serrano pepper, garlic, and ginger and cook for 30 seconds. Add the bay leaf and cinnamon stick, if using, and stir until well combined. Add the garam masala, salt, chili powder, turmeric, and coriander and stir continuously for 1 minute. Once the spices have been cooked down, add the tomatoes and kasoori methi, if using. Add the water, bring the gravy to a boil, and let simmer for 6 to 8 minutes. Some of the water should cook out as the sauce will thicken.

Place the eggs in the curry, cut sides up (for aesthetics!). Garnish with the cilantro, if using.

Keralan Egg Curry

2 tablespoons coriander seeds

2 tablespoons fennel seeds

1 tablespoon ground turmeric

1 tablespoon Kashmiri red chili powder

2 tablespoons coconut oil or neutral oil

2 tablespoons ginger paste *or* 2-inch
piece fresh ginger, grated

1 tablespoon garlic paste
or 3 garlic cloves, minced

1 or 2 green serrano peppers, minced

15 to 20 fresh curry leaves

2 medium white onions, finely diced

4 small Roma tomatoes, finely diced

1½ teaspoons salt

6 to 8 large eggs, hard-boiled (see
Ingredient Note on page 73),
peeled, and halved lengthwise

1 (13.5-ounce can) full-fat coconut milk

Fresh cilantro leaves, for garnish (optional)

✳ FREEZER NOTE

You can freeze the base sauce in an air-tight container for up to 3 months. Thaw in the fridge, then heat up on the stove, add the eggs, and let it simmer.

There are several regional versions of egg curry through-out India; this one, which hails from the south Indian state of Kerala, is simple to throw together. It's heavy on coconut milk and curry leaves, which work as a flavor-packed base for the hard-boiled eggs. But these ingredients also mean that this curry is a bit sweeter and much creamier than Punjabi Egg Curry (page 192). The recipe is modeled on a cozy and comforting version I had at Thattu, a restaurant in Chicago that specializes in Keralan cooking. I often make a big batch of this curry on a Sunday to eat throughout the week, with basmati rice or Simple Parathas (page 244).

In a small skillet, toast the coriander and fennel seeds over medium heat until fragrant, stirring constantly, about 3 minutes. Let the spices cool, then grind them into a powder using a spice grinder or a mortar and pestle. Add the turmeric and chili powder, mix well, and set aside.

In a large, heavy-bottomed pot or Dutch oven, melt the oil over medium heat. Add the ginger, garlic, serrano peppers, and curry leaves and cook for about 30 seconds, stirring frequently. Add the onions and let them cook until fragrant and soft, 10 to 12 minutes. Stir in the spice mixture so that the onions are coated and let cook for about 30 seconds, stirring frequently. Add the tomatoes and salt and let the mixture cook down until the tomatoes are soft and a lot of the water has cooked away, about 5 minutes.

Add the eggs, cut sides up (I like to arrange them in a cute cir-cle). Pour in the coconut milk and gently stir to combine. Turn the heat down to medium-low and cook for 8 to 10 minutes, stir-ring occasionally, until the eggs are heated through. If the curry is too thick for you, you can loosen it with a couple tablespoons of water. Garnish with cilantro, if using.

PUNJABI
EGG CURRY

KERALAN
EGG CURRY

Chana Masala

MASALA

1 tablespoon coriander seeds

1 dried red chile

1 whole clove

½-inch cinnamon stick

1 tablespoon cumin seeds, divided

¼ cup ghee or neutral oil

½ medium white onion, diced

1 tablespoon ginger paste *or* 1-inch
    piece fresh ginger, grated

1 tablespoon garlic paste
    or 3 garlic cloves, minced

1 bay leaf

½ (14-ounce) can crushed tomatoes

½ teaspoon amchur

½ teaspoon kala namak
    (black salt; optional)

1 (15-ounce) can chickpeas,
    drained and rinsed, *or* 1 cup dried
    chickpeas, cooked and drained

1 cup water

Salt to taste

2 green cardamom pods, smashed

1 tablespoon fresh lemon juice

Chopped fresh cilantro, for garnish

Sliced red onion, for serving

❄ FREEZER NOTE

Freeze any leftover chana masala in an
airtight container for up to 3 months. Thaw
in the fridge, then reheat in the microwave
or on the stovetop.

As far as crowd-pleasing dishes go, chana masala (also known as chole) checks off many boxes: the dish is vegetarian and vegan-friendly, quite cost effective, and really filling! It's hard to say no to perfectly stewed chickpeas in a comforting spiced-tomato sauce.

While it originates in north India, chana masala is beloved in most Indian households and can be found on most Indian restaurant menus. It's best served with lemon wedges on the side and topped with thin slices of red onion. Chana masala pairs well with a pot of Spinach Jeera Rice (page 152) and Cucumber Raita (page 64), and also with Simple Parathas (page 244) or Puri (page 253) if you're feeling celebratory. If you don't want to deal with toasting and grinding the spices yourself, most Indian grocery stores sell premade blends for chana masala that will work.

To make the masala, toast the coriander seeds, dried chile, clove, cinnamon stick, and ½ tablespoon cumin seeds in a small skillet over medium-high heat, stirring constantly, for about 2 minutes, or until the spices start to smell toasty. Grind the spices into a powder using a spice grinder or a mortar and pestle. Set aside.

Melt the ghee in a large, heavy-bottomed pot over medium heat. Add the remaining ½ tablespoon cumin seeds and let them pop, 20 to 30 seconds. Add the onion and cook for 2 to 3 minutes, until soft and almost translucent. Add the ginger, garlic, and bay leaf and cook, stirring occasionally, for 1 to 2 minutes. Add the crushed tomatoes and cook for 3 to 5 minutes, until the ghee starts to separate from the tomato-onion mixture. Stir in the toasted spice mixture, amchur, and kala namak, if using. Stir in the chickpeas and water, season with salt, and add the smashed cardamom. Bring to a simmer and cook for 5 to 7 minutes, until the liquid has reduced slightly. Stir in the lemon juice and cook for another 5 or so minutes. You want the chana masala to be saucy but not watery. Remove from the heat and garnish with cilantro. Serve with red onion slices.

ON CASTE

When it comes to Indian food in America, caste is not quite the elephant in the room—maybe it's closer to a lion or a grizzly bear—but it's something that needs to be acknowledged and discussed openly. Yes, even in a cookbook. Perhaps, especially in a cookbook.

There is so much that I love about my heritage and about Indian culture. I love eating with my hands, even if my nails occasionally undergo an involuntary turmeric stain manicure. I love the rich history of textiles, and the closet bursting with saris and lehengas at my parents' house. I love that my first cousins feel like my siblings and my second cousins like my first cousins. I love that I clap when I laugh, that my DNA viscerally craves mangoes at a certain point in the year, that Bollywood movies are often three hours long, and that certain words come to me in Hindi and Gujarati first, and English second. I find caste to be a dark shadow that looms over the warmth and inclusivity inherent in Indian culture, and a part of me was reluctant to give it a spotlight. But the caste system's reach and influence is everywhere, even if it is not obvious, and this includes how and what people eat.

Rooted in ancient India, the caste system is said to be over 3,000 years old. However, the influence of the system as it exists today really developed in the period between the downfall of the Mughal empire and the rise of British colonization in India. It divides Hindus into rigid hierarchical groups. There are five main ones, with the Brahmins at the top and the Dalits, also known as the "untouchables," at the very bottom, and the various castes further divided into nearly 3,000 subcastes.

Your caste dictated where you lived, who you could marry, and, yes, what you ate. Being upper caste often meant that you were a strict vegetarian to the point that the food could only be prepared in certain kitchens, by certain people. The lowest caste, or the Dalits, were left to eat what the higher castes did not want to consume—this often meant off-cuts of meat like offal and other foods that were considered "dirty." (A truly ridiculous system!) Technically, India outlawed the discrimination of people due to caste in 1948 and codified it into the constitution in 1950, but the effects are very much still felt in society today.

I grew up in straight-from-a-sitcom suburban Michigan, smack-dab in the middle of the state, surrounded by chain restaurants and churches. That means I went to school with more Katherines/ Katies/Katys than I could count, that no substitute teacher could ever get my name right, and, yes, that my lunches were considered "smelly." But it

AND FOOD

also means that I grew up with the immense privilege of being blissfully unaware of the caste system for a large part of my childhood until I heard someone mention it in middle school. Perhaps this is also because my family is Jain, a religion that technically does not fall within the caste system. (However, Jains tend to be well educated, and vegetarianism is the center of the Jain belief system, meaning they often did not face the same levels of discrimination as lower caste groups.) I've found that this is a common experience of many others who grew up as part of the Indian American diaspora: caste wasn't something we were confronted with every day.

This is not to say that the influence of caste does not exist in the diaspora. There are the few that cling to its toxic remnants: engaging in behaviors like demanding their children only wed someone from the same caste; or the handful of terrible cases coming out in Silicon Valley of workplace discrimination based on an immigrant employee's caste. For the most part, though, growing up in America, I felt that Indians tried to focus on the things that bonded us in diaspora, rather than the systems that divided us.

But it would be irresponsible to not acknowledge the influence the caste system has on the ways Indians eat in America today. While the American diaspora is not limited to upper-caste Indians only, those were often the only people with the resources to make the journey. (It's a very white collar–heavy diaspora, unlike the makeup of, say, the British Indian and Caribbean Indian diasporas.) And so many of the dishes in this book are grounded in upper-caste foodways—which also helps explain the diaspora's complicated and finicky relationship with meat (see Q & A on page 92). Please keep in mind that while I believe that everyone should be aware of the impact of caste, it remains an ideology that I am deeply uninterested in furthering. This book is meant to be a celebration and exploration of Indian American cooking—meant for everybody, regardless of caste or creed.

I am not even remotely an expert on caste. If you'd like to know more, I encourage you to read the following authors and experts who have written exceptionally well on such a challenging topic:

Anything by B. R. Ambedkar

Coming Out as Dalit by Yashica Dutt

Caste by Isabel Wilkerson

Caste Matters by Suraj Yengde

Mexican Pizza

FRIED TORTILLAS

¼ cup neutral oil, for frying

8 flour tortillas

BEANS

1 (15-ounce) can refried pinto beans

¼ cup water

2 tablespoons taco seasoning

½ small white onion, diced

TOPPINGS

1 (10-ounce) can enchilada sauce

2 cups shredded Mexican cheese blend

1 Roma tomato diced

1 scallion, chopped

Pickled jalapeños (optional)

Sliced black olives (optional)

If there is one thing that bonds Indian families in America, it is Taco Bell. The fast-food chain is a cultural obsession. An Indian wedding isn't valid until someone has gone through the Taco Bell drive-thru at midnight for dozens of bean burritos and Mexican pizzas for the after-party. It's really the only place my family ate (and still eats) on road trips. Every Indian has their go-to order (mine is a Crunchwrap Supreme, no beef, sub beans, and a Cheesy Bean and Rice Burrito, add red sauce). And most households have Taco Bell sauce packets stuffed into corners of random drawers, or collected in a big ziplock bag. I always keep bottles of the Taco Bell mild sauce in my fridge. At this point, Taco Bell is Indian food.

Many have theorized why Indians love Taco Bell: it's very vegetarian-friendly given that you can swap out any meat for beans, there's some spice to the food, and tortillas aren't so different from rotis and parathas. At this point, Taco Bell should be considered Indian food—especially the Mexican Pizza, which remains a community favorite. So much so that when Taco Bell made the mistake of taking it off the menu, an Indian American superfan, Krish Jagirdar, launched an online petition that gained over 170,000 signatures, convincing the chain to bring the Mexican Pizza back permanently. This recipe is based on the Mexican Pizza that Taco Bell used to sell that was topped with slices of black olives and diced scallions, but you can leave them off if you want. I prefer to *live más.*

Preheat the oven to 400 degrees F. Line a rimmed baking sheet with aluminum foil or parchment paper.

In a large skillet, heat the oil over medium heat. Add 1 tortilla and lightly fry, flipping frequently, until the tortilla is golden brown and crisp, about 3 minutes. Set on a plate lined with paper towels and repeat with the remaining tortillas.

Recipe continues

Now amp up the beans: In a medium saucepan, heat the canned beans and water over medium heat. Stir in the taco seasoning and onion, mix well, and remove from the heat.

Place 1 fried tortilla on the prepared baking sheet and spread on one-quarter of the beans. Drizzle with a tablespoon or so of enchilada sauce, then add a second tortilla on top. Spread on another layer of enchilada sauce, then sprinkle with one-quarter each of the cheese, diced tomato, scallions, pickled jalapeños, and black olives, if using. Repeat to make 3 more Mexican pizzas. Bake until the cheese is melted, 4 to 6 minutes. Slice into quarters and serve.

Pav Bhaji

QUICK PAV BHAJI MASALA

1 tablespoon Garam Masala (page 62)

2 teaspoons Kashmiri red chili powder

2 teaspoons amchur

1 teaspoon ground turmeric

1 teaspoon ground coriander

1 teaspoon ground cumin

½ teaspoon ground cinnamon

½ teaspoon ground cardamom

2 tablespoons neutral oil or ghee

1 large white onion, minced

3 or 4 Roma tomatoes, chopped, *or*

    ½ (14-ounce) can crushed tomatoes

4 medium red potatoes, boiled

    until mashable and peeled

½ head cauliflower, boiled until mashable

1 cup frozen green peas, boiled until mashable

Salt to taste

1 to 2 cups water

1 tablespoon unsalted butter,

    plus more for the bread

4 to 8 potato rolls or hamburger buns

Lemon wedges, for serving

Sliced onion, for serving

How did one of Mumbai's most famous street foods—the ultimate late-night snack—become an easy weeknight dinner in America? Pav bhaji consists of toasted bread (pav) and mashed, seasoned vegetables (bhaji), plus plenty of butter (but they for some reason left that out of the name). People like to describe it as "Indian sloppy joes," and while visually they have similarities, the taste could not be more different.

At its simplest, pav bhaji is made from mashed potatoes and peas, cooked in a tomato-onion gravy and then heavily seasoned. If you have other vegetables on hand that mash well, feel free to throw them in: cauliflower, eggplant, carrots, green beans. If you have a freezer stocked with frozen vegetables, this is the dish to make when last-minute guests come over.

Instead of pav, a type of soft bread roll whose origins are rooted in the Portuguese colonization of India's western coast, my recipe calls for griddled potato rolls or hamburger buns. The best way to serve pav bhaji is with lemon wedges and a mountain of raw onions. There is a running joke in my family that I eat my onions with a little bit of bhaji.

In a small bowl, combine all of the quick pav bhaji masala ingredients; set aside.

In a large pot, heat the oil over medium heat. Add the onion and sauté for 2 to 3 minutes, until it begins to soften, then add the tomatoes. Let the mixture cook down until the tomatoes start to get jammy and the oil starts to separate from the mixture, 7 to 8 minutes. Add the potatoes, cauliflower, and peas and gently mash them into the tomato gravy—I prefer to leave some small pieces of the vegetables so the mash has some texture. Add the

Recipe continues

✿ INGREDIENT NOTE

If you don't want to make the pav bhaji masala, you can easily buy a premade version at most Indian grocery stores or online. Just replace the quick pav bhaji masala from the recipe with about 2 tablespoons of the premade masala blend.

❄ FREEZER NOTE

Leftover bhaji will keep in an airtight container in the freezer for at least 3 months.

pav bhaji masala, salt, and 1 cup water and stir. Bring the mixture to a simmer and let the flavors meld for about 10 minutes, then turn off the heat, cover, and let it sit for 5 to 10 minutes. Add up to 1 cup more water if needed; you want the texture to be like sloppy joes—spoonable but not thick.

Heat a large skillet or griddle over medium heat. Spread a generous amount of butter on the cut sides of each roll and griddle them until the bread is lightly toasted, about 1 minute.

Pop the remaining 1 tablespoon butter into the mashed vegetable mixture and stir until it melts. I like to squeeze several lemon wedges over the vegetables and top with a proper flourish of raw onions before piling it onto a griddled roll.

Khichdi

½ cup long-grain white rice (not basmati)

½ cup moong dal, preferably without skin

2½ cups water

2 teaspoons salt

1 teaspoon ground turmeric

1 teaspoon Kashmiri red chili powder

TADKA

1½ tablespoons ghee or neutral oil

½ teaspoon black mustard seeds

4 whole cloves

1-inch cinnamon stick

❄ **FREEZER NOTE**

You can freeze khichdi in an airtight container for at least 3 months. Just thaw and reheat in the microwave.

If any of the recent glut of wellness articles about khichdi are to be believed, the dish will detox you and cure everything. While yes, khichdi does have several health benefits—I can't argue that it isn't nourishing—it is, and has always been, way more than a health food.

What makes khichdi, well, khichdi is the cooking of the rice and lentils together, along with a handful of spices. It's an incredibly versatile meal, what I eat after long trips, or when I feel a cold coming on, or when I just need something warm and easy. Some people like their khichdi to be soupy, but I find the texture so much more satisfying when the khichdi skews drier. I eat it with ghee folded in and a spoonful of Indian mango pickle, or swimming in a lake of Gujarati Kadhi (page 217).

If you don't have an Instant Pot, preheat the oven to 350 degrees F.

In a medium bowl, combine the rice and dal. Rinse and drain the mixture at least 3 times, until the water runs clear. Add the water, salt, turmeric, and chili powder and give it a good mix.

To make the tadka, in a small saucepan, heat the ghee over medium heat. Add the mustard seeds and let them pop for 5 to 10 seconds, then remove the pan from the heat and add the cloves and cinnamon stick. Let it cool for 2 minutes.

If you have an Instant Pot, pour the tadka into the rice mixture and give it a hefty stir until everything is well combined. Transfer to the Instant Pot and cook on high pressure for 7 minutes.

If you don't have an Instant Pot, add the rice mixture to the tadka in the saucepan, stir, and bring to a boil over high heat. Cover tightly and bake for 5 minutes, then turn off the oven but do not open the oven door! Let it sit for 2 hours undisturbed before serving.

GUJARATI KADHI
(PAGE 217)

Dal Makhani

1 cup whole urad dal (with the skin)

¼ cup dry kidney beans

7 cups water, divided

3 tablespoons unsalted butter

2 tablespoons ghee

½ medium yellow onion, diced

1 tablespoon garlic paste
   or 3 garlic cloves, minced

1 tablespoon ginger paste or 1–inch
   piece fresh ginger, grated

1 teaspoon Garam Masala (page 62)

½ teaspoon Kashmiri red chili powder

1 bay leaf

2 Roma tomatoes, diced, or ½ (14–ounce)
   can crushed tomatoes

2 teaspoons salt

1 cup water

¼ cup half-and-half

2 tablespoons kasoori methi (optional)

❄ **FREEZER NOTE**

Dal makhani freezes incredibly well. Divide leftovers into individual-serving airtight containers and use within 3 or 4 months.

🍴 **EXTRA CREDIT**

I've also seen a handful of restaurants serve dal makhani with a full ball of burrata in the center, which seems both unnecessary and brilliant.

"Makhani" indicates that something has a generous amount of butter in it, and while this dish is true to its name, it's not the butter (nor the half-and-half) that makes this dish luxurious. Those ingredients make it rich. What makes it luxurious is the way the lentils and kidney beans cook down into a texture so tender and velvety that you have no choice but to stop and admire the bowl in front of you. It's impossible to eat dal makhani in a rush. It demands that you pause, even if the world around you does not.

You will find dal makhani (sometimes labeled "black dal") on the menu of any Indian restaurant that serves northern Indian food, and their versions tend to be heavier because of the amount of cream they pour in. My version uses half-and-half and a mixture of ghee and butter because I like the rich flavor the combination imparts. And since it calls for so much, definitely use the good butter! Eat over rice or with Super Flaky Parathas (page 247) or Simple Parathas (page 244).

Soak the urad dal and kidney beans in a bowl of water for at least 8 hours, or overnight. Drain, then transfer to an Instant Pot, add 6 cups fresh water, and cook on high pressure for 30 minutes.

Meanwhile, in a large, heavy-bottomed pot, melt the butter and ghee over low heat. Add the onion and cook for 4 minutes, until softened but not brown. Stir in the garlic, ginger, garam masala, chili powder, and bay leaf and cook for 30 seconds, then add the tomatoes and salt and cook for 2 minutes. Add the dal and kidney bean mixture with the cooking water, plus the remaining 1 cup fresh water, and bring to a boil. It should not be super liquidy at this point. Let the dal simmer with the lid ajar for 30 minutes, or until it has gently thickened. Stir in the half-and-half and remove from the heat. Add the kasoori methi, if using.

Spinach Tadka Dal

1 cup moong dal (preferably skinless)

4½ cups water, divided

1 tablespoon ghee

2 teaspoons cumin seeds

1 small white onion, diced

2 small Roma tomatoes, diced

1 tablespoon ginger paste *or* 1–inch piece fresh ginger, grated

1½ teaspoons garlic paste *or* 2 garlic cloves, minced (optional)

2 teaspoons salt

1½ teaspoons ground turmeric

1 teaspoon Kashmiri red chili powder

1 cup chopped fresh spinach

1 lemon, juiced

1 tablespoon Chaat Masala (page 63)

✳ FREEZER NOTE

The cooked dal will keep in an airtight container in the freezer for at least 3 months. Thaw at room temp and reheat on the stove or in the microwave.

If you find cooking lentils intimidating, this recipe is for you. It's one of the simplest dal recipes in existence and very, very difficult to mess up as long as you have an Instant Pot or stovetop pressure cooker. It's one of those back-pocket recipes that is as reliable as that pair of boots you have worn for 10 years. I love to throw a few handfuls of spinach into the dal to add color and make it a more complete meal, served with white rice. If you use oil instead of ghee, it's also one of those dishes that's great for a crowd with dietary restrictions.

Wash and rinse the dal 3 times, until the water runs clear. Drain the dal and put it in the Instant Pot, along with 2½ cups fresh water. Cook on high pressure for 4 minutes.

Meanwhile, in a Dutch over or other large, heavy-bottomed pot, melt the ghee over medium heat. Add the cumin seeds and let them pop, then add the onion and tomatoes and give it a good stir. Turn the heat up to medium and cook, stirring occasionally, for 4 to 5 minutes, until the onion is soft. Add the ginger and garlic, if using, and give it a stir. Add the salt, turmeric, and chili powder and mix well. Add the spinach and remaining 2 cups water and let it simmer for 7 to 8 minutes, until the spinach is fully wilted.

Gently mix the dal, then add it to the pot with the spinach mixture and stir.

Chili Paneer Dumplings

SAUCE

2 ½ tablespoons soy sauce

2 ½ tablespoons ketchup

1 tablespoon sriracha or chili garlic sauce

1 ½ teaspoons rice vinegar

1 teaspoon Kashmiri red chili powder

½ teaspoon ground black pepper

DUMPLINGS

2 tablespoons neutral oil, plus
   more for cooking dumplings

½ medium white onion, chopped

1 ½ teaspoons garlic paste *or* 2
   garlic cloves, minced

1 ½ teaspoons ginger paste *or* ½-inch
   piece fresh ginger, grated

½ red bell pepper, chopped

½ green bell pepper, chopped

8 ounces paneer, crumbled or shredded

1 ½ teaspoons cornstarch

2 tablespoons water, plus more
   for cooking the dumplings

2 scallions, green parts only,
   sliced on the bias

1 (12– to 14–ounce) package
   square wonton wrappers

This dish is an amalgamation of two of the best snacks of all time: chili paneer and momos. The former is an Indo-Chinese staple, where cubes of fried paneer with a furiously crunchy exterior are tossed in a sticky sauce that is sweet and sour and spicy—it's easy to eat a whole plate by yourself. The latter are a style of steamed dumpling that are extremely popular in north India, Nepal, and beyond—it's also easy to eat a whole plate of these by yourself. I figured why not combine the two into one kick-ass dish—the best of both worlds. These dumplings go perfectly with a batch of Hakka Noodles (page 165) and a bowl of Cauliflower Manchurian (page 240).

In a small bowl, whisk together all of the sauce ingredients; set aside.

To make the dumplings, heat the oil in a medium skillet over medium heat. Add the onion and cook until it starts to turn translucent, about 2 minutes. Add the garlic and ginger and cook for 1 minute, then add the bell peppers and cook for 1 to 2 minutes, until the peppers start to soften. Add the sauce, stir to combine, and let cook for 30 to 60 seconds. Fold in the paneer and keep stirring the mixture to cook out any remaining water, 3 to 4 minutes.

In a small bowl, whisk together the cornstarch and water and pour the mixture over the paneer filling. Remove the pan from the heat, add the scallions, and give everything a quick mix. Set the filling aside until it is completely cool before you start filling your dumplings!

Recipe continues

Keep a small bowl of water to the side. Add about 2 teaspoons of filling to the center of a wonton wrapper. Wet two adjacent edges of the wrapper and bring the two dry edges over the filling so that they line up with the wet edges. Press them together, forming a triangle. Make sure there are no air bubbles. Bring the two bottom corners of the triangle together, wet one edge, and press the edges together to form a wonton shape. Repeat to fill as many dumplings as you can with the filling.

To cook the dumplings, heat a little bit of oil in a large skillet over medium-high heat. Add 8 to 10 dumplings, or as many as will fit comfortably in a single layer in your pan, and cook for 3 to 4 minutes, until the bottoms start to brown. Add about ¼ cup water to the pan and immediately cover with a lid to let the dumplings steam for 2 to 3 minutes, until all the water has cooked off. The dumplings should be soft and the skins gently translucent. Remove the lid and let the dumplings cook for another 1 to 2 minutes, uncovered. Repeat to cook the remaining dumplings. Serve with soy sauce or spicy cilantro chutney for dipping.

Saag Paneer

1 pound baby spinach

2 small Roma tomatoes, quartered

2 green serrano peppers, cut in half

1 bunch cilantro, leaves only

3 tablespoons kasoori methi (optional but highly encouraged)

3 tablespoons ghee or neutral oil

1 medium white onion, finely chopped

1½ tablespoons garlic paste
   or 5 garlic cloves, minced

1½ tablespoons ginger paste
   or 1½-inch piece fresh ginger, grated

1½ tablespoons ground coriander

2 teaspoons ground cumin

1½ teaspoons Kashmiri red chili powder

1 teaspoon ground turmeric

Salt to taste

¾ cup water

1 (12-ounce) block paneer,
   cut into 1-inch cubes

❄ FREEZER NOTE

Saag paneer is very freezer-friendly. Divide up leftovers into individual-serving airtight containers and freeze for up to 3 months. Reheat in the microwave or in a pot on the stove over low heat.

🍴 EXTRA CREDIT

I like to use leftovers to make frittatas (page 26), as a base sauce for naan pizza (page 149), and in lasagna (page 169).

Saag paneer is perhaps the most delicious way to get yourself to consume a boatload of leafy greens. They're cooked down until they form a silky sauce that is tossed with cubes of cheese—what is not to love?

You might see this dish called palak paneer on certain menus and saag paneer on others. "Palak" refers to a dish made from just spinach, while "saag" refers to a mix of leafy greens—like spinach, mustard greens, and even Swiss chard. In this recipe, I use mostly spinach plus a little bit of cilantro and dried fenugreek leaves out of convenience, but feel free to mix and match. I also find it vital to blend the greens—some do not—but the texture of the sauce is much more velvety if you do. It also helps the sauce feel creamy without the addition of any dairy.

The dish pairs extremely well with both Super Flaky Parathas (page 247) and Simple Parathas (page 244), as well as white rice.

Bring a large pot of water to a boil, then add the spinach. As soon as the greens fully wilt (about 2 minutes), drain the spinach in a colander and run it under cold water. Let drain; there is no need to squeeze the water out.

Transfer the spinach to a blender, along with the tomatoes, serrano peppers, cilantro leaves, and kasoori methi (if using) and blitz until very smooth—it should have the consistency of one those bright green smoothies that looks a little too healthy. Set aside.

In a large, heavy-bottomed pot or Dutch oven, melt the ghee over medium heat. Add the onion and sauté for 6 to 7 minutes, until softened and somewhat golden. Add the garlic and ginger and cook, stirring, for 2 minutes. Add the coriander, cumin, chili powder, turmeric, and salt and give it a good stir. Add the spinach mixture, water, and paneer cubes and let the mixture simmer for 10 to 12 minutes, stirring occasionally, until the sauce is slightly thickened.

Gujarati Kadhi

KADHI

1½ cups plain full-fat yogurt
  (the sourer, the better)

2¼ cups water

¼ cup besan flour

1 teaspoon salt

3 tablespoons sugar

½ teaspoon cumin seeds

½-inch piece fresh ginger, grated

½ green serrano pepper, minced

¼ teaspoon ground cardamom

Handful chopped fresh cilantro,
  for garnish (optional)

TADKA

1 teaspoon ghee

½ teaspoon mustard seeds

½ teaspoon fenugreek seeds (optional)

1-inch cinnamon stick

4 whole cloves

20 to 25 fresh curry leaves (optional)

Pinch Kashmiri red chili powder

❄ **FREEZER NOTE**
You can freeze kadhi in an airtight container for up to 3 months. Just reheat on the stovetop.

It's not always possible to stuff Indian dishes into Western culinary categories. While kadhi, which is made from yogurt and besan (gram) flour, is brothy, it isn't a broth, or a soup, or a stew. Kadhi is simply kadhi. It's wonderfully soothing and is eaten throughout northern India. There are, of course, different regional styles, but I am partial to Gujarati kadhi, which has two signature characteristics: it tends to be light in color (because most people make it without turmeric), and it tends to be sweeter than other kadhi styles (this is very typical of Gujarati cooking generally). I find the sweetness comforting, but if you're worried about it, feel free to cut the sugar down to 2 tablespoons. You can enjoy kadhi with just a scoop of plain white rice or with Khichdi (page 206). If you're in the mood to whip up a feast, a pot of kadhi is delicious alongside freshly fried Puri (page 253) and a bowl of Shrikhand (page 291).

In a large, heavy-bottomed pot, blend the yogurt and water together until smooth, either whisking by hand or using an immersion blender. Add the besan flour and salt and reblend until super smooth. Add the sugar, cumin seeds, ginger, and serrano pepper and give it a stir. Bring the mixture to a boil over high heat, then turn the heat down to a simmer.

To make the tadka, in a small saucepan, melt the ghee over medium heat. Add the mustard seeds; once they start to pop, carefully add the fenugreek seeds (if using) and remove the pan from the heat. Stir in the cinnamon, cloves, curry leaves (if using), and chili powder.

Add the tadka to the yogurt mixture and bring back to a boil over medium-high heat. Add the cardamom and let it gently boil for about 5 minutes. Remove from the heat and top with the cilantro, if using.

Spicy Cilantro Chutney Mussels

2 pounds fresh mussels
   (see Ingredient Note)
1 tablespoon neutral oil
1 scallion, chopped
1½ tablespoons garlic paste
   or 5 garlic cloves, minced
1 tablespoon ginger paste *or* 1-inch
   piece fresh ginger, grated
½ cup Spicy Cilantro Chutney (page 51)
1 (13.5-ounce) can coconut milk
½ cup water
1 teaspoon sugar
1 teaspoon salt
Juice of 1 lime

🌿 INGREDIENT NOTE
You can use frozen mussels instead of fresh; follow the directions on the package for thawing.

❄ FREEZER NOTE
The broth, without the mussels, will keep in an airtight container in the freezer for up to 3 months.

This recipe was inspired by a game of "What can I make for dinner with the things in my overstuffed freezer?" Spicy Cilantro Chutney (page 51) freezes incredibly well, so I always have some on hand. That plus aromatics like a ton of garlic and ginger, plus a can of coconut milk, and I had dinner ready in basically the same amount of time it takes for drama to burst out on an episode of the *Real Housewives* (a mere few minutes). For those who prefer to eat more plant-based, I recommend simmering coins of king oyster mushrooms in this broth and serving it over rice. Either way, serve with rice, Super Flaky Parathas (page 247), Tadka Focaccia (page 258), or just some good crusty bread.

Rinse the mussels very well under cold running water until there is no visible dirt and scrape off any barnacles. Debeard the mussels (the hairy fibers where the mussels attach to things) and make sure to throw out any mussels that have cracked shells or are open, which means they are likely dead and you risk serious gastric distress or even food poisoning.

In a large saucepan, heat the oil over medium heat. Add the scallion, garlic, and ginger and cook for 1 to 2 minutes, until the scallion is softened. Stir in the chutney, coconut milk, water, sugar, and salt and bring to a simmer, stirring occasionally. Let the mixture simmer for 4 to 5 minutes, then add the lime juice and mussels. Cover and let the mussels steam until they open, 2 to 6 minutes; please throw out any that do not open because they are likely dead. Transfer the mussels to a large bowl and spoon the broth over them.

VEGET

While I love a big bowl of lettuce, Indian cuisine isn't known for its leafy salad culture—there isn't exactly a desi Sweetgreen—but spendy salads aren't the only delicious way to eat your vegetables. Cooked vegetables are foundational to Indian home cooking—often simple in nature, but not in flavor.

VEGETABLES

Cabbage Nu Shaak

1½ tablespoons neutral oil

½ head green cabbage, shredded

1 teaspoon salt

1 teaspoon ground turmeric

¾ teaspoon Kashmiri red chili powder

🍲 STORAGE NOTE

This does not freeze well. Leftovers keep in an airtight container in the fridge for a couple of days.

When people say that Indian food is "too complicated" and requires "too many ingredients," I like to point to this simple cabbage stir-fry. It's one of the many dishes my incredible mother, a busy dentist, would whip up on a weeknight after a long day of work. As an adult, I make this dish almost weekly, usually mixed with a scoop of white rice and a hefty spoonful of plain yogurt, or with Simple Parathas (page 244). It requires only two spices (if you don't include salt) and takes mere minutes to make.

Heat the oil in a large skillet over high heat. Add the cabbage, salt, and turmeric and mix well. Sauté for about 5 minutes, stirring constantly, until the cabbage is tender. Stir in the chili powder and cook for another minute.

Aloo Gobi

3 tablespoons neutral oil

1½ teaspoons black mustard seeds

2 teaspoons ground coriander

1½ teaspoons ground turmeric

1½ teaspoons Kashmiri red chili powder

1 teaspoon salt

¼ teaspoon hing (asafoetida; optional)

5 small red potatoes, peeled and
   cut into ½-inch pieces

½ head cauliflower, cut into small florets

2 to 3 tablespoons kasoori methi or
   chopped fresh cilantro (optional)

❄ FREEZER NOTE

You can freeze aloo gobi in an airtight container for up to 3 months. Thaw it in the fridge overnight before reheating.

Whenever I eat aloo gobi, I can't help but think of the iconic line in the movie *Bend It Like Beckham* when the main character, Jess, frustratedly declares, "Anyone can cook aloo gobi, but who can bend the ball like Beckham?" And she is right, anyone really *can* cook aloo gobi. The simple dish of stir-fried potatoes (aloo) and cauliflower (gobi) is quick Indian home cooking at its most comforting.

I like to use red potatoes because of how tender they are, but russet potatoes (or any potato, really) will also work well. Make sure the potato pieces and the cauliflower florets are about the same size, or the florets will feel soggy. If you don't want to use or don't have hing, you can add a bit of garlic paste or minced garlic to the recipe. Make it a weeknight dinner with some Simple Parathas (page 244) and Classic Kachumber (page 226).

In a large, heavy-bottomed pot, heat the oil over medium heat. Add the mustard seeds and let them pop, about 30 seconds. Turn the heat down to low and add the coriander, turmeric, chili powder, salt, and hing (if using). Give the spices a stir and then quickly add the potatoes and cauliflower. Stir until each piece is coated with the oil and spice mixture. Turn the heat up to medium-low, cover, and cook for 7 minutes undisturbed. (It's tempting to take off the lid and stir, but please wait until the 7 minutes are up.)

Uncover and stir every few minutes until the potatoes are fork-tender, about 18 minutes. Remove the pan from the heat and top with the kasoori methi or cilantro, if using.

Okra Masala

2 tablespoons neutral oil

1 pound okra (see Ingredient Note),
   cut into ¼-inch pieces

2 teaspoons ground coriander

1 teaspoon salt

½ teaspoon Kashmiri red chili powder

½ teaspoon ground cumin

❧ INGREDIENT NOTE

You can use fresh or frozen okra, but if using frozen, you need to up the cooking time by 3 to 5 minutes.

🥣 STORAGE NOTE

Okra masala doesn't freeze well, but you can store it in an airtight container in the fridge for up to 3 days. Reheat in the microwave.

My mom, Hina, is an incredibly smart woman who has taught me many tips and tricks in life, but my favorite one of them all might be this: the key to crispy, not slimy, okra masala is to use the microwave. I know microwave cooking gets a bad rap, but if you utilize it correctly, it can be one of the most useful tools in the kitchen. Case in point: this dish. It offers a relatively hands-off method of cooking okra that avoids deep-frying but still results in something that is a far cry from a mushy and "sad" microwave dinner.

It might seem aggressive to microwave a vegetable for nearly half an hour in total, but I promise the final texture is worth it. And since you are not stir-frying the okra, known as bhindi in Hindi, your hands are free to make a batch of Gujarati Kadhi (page 217) and Simple Parathas (page 244) to serve alongside.

Heat the oil in a microwave-safe bowl for 1 minute. Add the okra, coriander, salt, chili powder, and cumin and give it a good stir so that the okra is evenly coated and the spices are well distributed. Cover and cook in the microwave on high for 8 minutes. Remove from the microwave and stir the okra again. Re-cover and microwave for another 8 minutes, then stir again. Repeat these steps 2 more times, until the okra has cooked in the microwave for about 32 minutes. If you like your okra a bit crispier, feel free to microwave it for an additional 3 to 7 minutes.

Malai Broccoli

½ cup plain full-fat Greek yogurt

4 ounces full-fat cream cheese, at room temperature

1½ teaspoons garlic paste *or* 2 garlic cloves, minced

1½ teaspoons ginger paste *or* ½-inch piece fresh ginger, grated

½ teaspoon Garam Masala (page 62)

½ teaspoon white pepper

¼ teaspoon ground black pepper

¼ teaspoon ground cardamom

¼ teaspoon sugar

Salt to taste

1 large head broccoli, cut into florets (about 4 cups)

Neutral oil, for greasing (optional)

🍲 STORAGE NOTE

Malai broccoli does not freeze well. Leftovers can stay in an airtight container in the fridge for up to 2 days; reheat in the oven so that the broccoli does not become soggy.

A pet peeve of mine is when recipes make these exaggerated claims that they'll get you to love a food you hate. The reality is no amount of cream cheese or spices will make you love broccoli if you hate broccoli. But if you're someone who can tolerate broccoli but doesn't love it yet, this recipe might make you obsessed with the cruciferous vegetable.

Somehow, nearly every vegetable tastes better once it is marinated in yogurt (and in this case, cream cheese, too). The creamy and tangy coating makes roasted broccoli infinitely more interesting and rich in texture and flavor. The method is like how one might make tandoori chicken or paneer, but the spice profile leans a little sweeter and more peppery. I know the recipe says it serves 4 to 6 people, but I often make a batch and eat it alone for dinner. This is a good back-pocket marinade for several other vegetables, including sweet potatoes, butternut squash, and carrots.

In a medium bowl, mix the yogurt and cream cheese and stir until smooth, with no lumps. Mix in the garlic, ginger, garam masala, white pepper, black pepper, cardamom, sugar, and salt until well combined. Add the broccoli and toss to coat. Cover and let the broccoli marinate in the fridge for at least 30 minutes, but ideally a couple of hours.

Preheat the oven to 450 degrees F. Coat a rimmed baking sheet with a thin layer of oil or a sheet of parchment paper.

Spread the broccoli evenly across the prepared baking sheet and bake for 20 to 25 minutes, flipping the florets halfway through, until the broccoli is tender. Move the baking sheet up to the top rack, turn the oven to broil, and broil the broccoli for 2 to 3 minutes, watching closely so that the florets develop a light char and crispy edges but do not burn.

Masala Smashed Potatoes

1½ pounds mixed baby or
  small red potatoes
3 tablespoons olive oil, divided
1½ teaspoons garlic paste
  or 2 garlic cloves, minced
1 teaspoon Chaat Masala (page 63)
½ teaspoon Garam Masala (page 62)
¼ teaspoon Kashmiri red chili powder
¼ teaspoon ground coriander
Salt and ground black pepper to taste
Juice of 1 small lemon
Chopped scallions, for garnish
Handful fresh cilantro leaves, for garnish
Sour cream, for serving

🥣 STORAGE NOTE

Cooked potatoes do not freeze well, but they will keep in an airtight container in the fridge for a couple of days. Reheat in an oven or air fryer to maintain their crispiness.

Smashed potatoes are essentially roasted potatoes but with even more texture. Thanks to the increased surface area, smashed potatoes have unbelievably crispy edges, fluffy and creamy interiors, and paper-thin crackly skin. Also, it's deeply satisfying to smash down a potato—scratches that same itch as popping bubble wrap.

I love seasoning potatoes with a mix of chaat and garam masala and a ton of garlic. I personally double or triple the garlic I call for in this recipe. While these potatoes are delicious served with a bit of sour cream or Greek yogurt, you could also dunk them in Cilantro-Mint Chutney (page 50) or drizzle with Spicy Cilantro Chutney (page 51) if you like a bit of kick.

Bring a large pot of water to a boil. Add the potatoes and cook for about 20 minutes, until fork-tender. Drain the potatoes and let them cool for 2 to 3 minutes.

Preheat the oven to 450 degrees F. Coat a rimmed baking sheet with 1 tablespoon olive oil. (You want a good amount of oil on the baking sheet because that is what helps the potatoes get those delicious crispy edges.)

Transfer the potatoes to the prepared baking sheet and use a fork, the bottom of a heavy glass, or your palm to smash each potato so that it flattens. Be careful not to smash them too hard so that they break into multiple pieces. This process is definitely more fun than therapy!

In a bowl, combine the remaining 2 tablespoons olive oil, garlic, chaat masala, garam masala, chili powder, coriander, salt, and pepper and mix well. Brush the mixture generously onto each potato so that the surface of each spud is coated well. Bake for 30 to 35 minutes, until the potatoes are golden and crispy. Squeeze the lemon juice all over the potatoes. Garnish with scallions and cilantro and serve with a bowl of sour cream for dipping.

Endive and Paneer Salad
with Tamarind Chutney Vinaigrette

TAMARIND CHUTNEY VINAIGRETTE

½ cup Tamarind Chutney (page 52)

½ cup neutral oil

¼ cup water

Juice of ½ lemon

½ shallot, minced

SALAD

2 teaspoons neutral oil

3 ounces paneer, cut into ½-inch cubes

1 (5- to 6-ounce) package Little
   Gem lettuce, baby romaine,
   or romaine lettuce hearts

1 head endive, leaves separated

1 shallot, sliced into thin rings

2 tablespoons seasoned bread
   crumbs, toasted

🥣 STORAGE NOTE

Don't freeze the salad, but the dressing will keep in an airtight container in the fridge for at least a week.

Right after I graduated college, there was this short-lived and, quite frankly, not well executed Chipotle-style Indian bowl restaurant five blocks away from the apartment I was subletting in the financial district in New York City. It was affordable and filling and hit my cravings for Indian flavors on the regular. It was one of those places where you picked your starch (I always chose rice), your protein (always paneer), various toppings (lots of lettuce, raw onions, and tomatoes), and a sauce of your choice.

One time they were out of my go-to, so I settled for tamarind chutney. It was far too sweet and nearly ruined my bowl, but I found myself thinking that tamarind chutney could be the base for a good salad dressing. It was a question of adding more acid, and a fat to balance it out.

Since tamarind chutney is on the sweeter end, I like to use it to counter a bitter leaf like endive. Fry the paneer cubes right before serving so that they do not become chewy or hard. You could easily use halloumi cheese instead of paneer. The dressing and salad come together quickly, if you have the chutney on hand.

Combine all of the vinaigrette ingredients in a jar, cover, and shake until well combined. Set aside.

Heat the oil in a large skillet over medium heat. Add the paneer and cook for 3 to 4 minutes on each side, until lightly browned. Transfer the paneer to a plate and let it cool for a few minutes. While the paneer is cooling, arrange the lettuce and endive leaves on a large platter. Evenly spread the shallot rings on top, then scatter the paneer and bread crumbs over everything just before serving. Dress with a couple tablespoons of the vinaigrette.

Indian Tomato Soup

4 medium tomatoes

1 small potato, peeled

1 medium carrot, peeled

2 bay leaves

2-inch cinnamon stick *or*
  ½ teaspoon ground cinnamon

2 whole cloves

2 ½ cups water or vegetable broth

2 teaspoons neutral oil

½ teaspoon cumin seeds

2 teaspoons sugar

2 teaspoons salt

½ teaspoon ground black pepper

½ teaspoon Kashmiri red chili powder

Splash heavy cream, for serving (optional)

❄ **FREEZER NOTE**

This soup freezes well. Divide the soup between airtight individual-serving containers and freeze for up to 3 months. Reheat in the microwave or in a pot on the stove.

The very moment the weather starts to shift and the first chill hits the air, or I feel a gentle tickle in my throat, I immediately want a bowl of this tomato soup, a recipe my mom would always make for me. It's nothing like what you might get out of a Campbell's can. Indian tomato soup is much brothier and jazzed up with bay leaves (yes, they do serve a purpose!), cumin seeds, and Kashmiri red chili powder. The soup also has a touch of sweetness to it, thanks to the cinnamon and a pinch of sugar, which round out the flavor notes. The cream is optional at the end, but I wouldn't skip it, as it makes the bowl feel luxurious. You can also add a few croutons to the bowl, but I recommend whipping up a side of Masala Roasted Garlic Bread (page 261) or Tadka Focaccia (page 258) instead.

Combine the tomatoes, potato, carrot, bay leaves, cinnamon, cloves, and water in an Instant Pot and cook on high pressure for 5 minutes, until everything is tender. If you don't have an Instant Pot, combine the tomatoes, potato, carrots, bay leaves, cinnamon, cloves, and water in a large pot and bring to a boil. Cover, turn the heat down to a simmer, and cook for about 30 minutes, until everything is really super tender and easy to mash.

Remove the bay leaves, cinnamon, and cloves, transfer the vegetables and liquid to a blender, and blitz until smooth.

Heat the oil in a large, heavy-bottomed pot over medium heat. Add the cumin seeds and let them sizzle for 10 to 20 seconds. Pour in the tomato mixture and stir, then add the sugar, salt, black pepper, and chili powder. Bring the soup to a boil, then turn the heat down to a simmer and cook for 4 to 5 minutes. Ladle into bowls and add a drizzle of cream, if using.

TADKA FOCACCIA (PAGE 258)

Most Indian breads are flat, but that doesn't mean they aren't exciting. Have you ever watched a puri puff in hot oil? There are few things in this world that are more satisfying. The best part about flatbreads is that they don't require an oven—or much patience. Who doesn't love instant gratification, especially in the form of carbohydrates?

BR

EADS

Simple Parathas

1½ cups whole wheat flour (atta),
   plus more for dusting

1 teaspoon salt

½ teaspoon cumin seeds

1 tablespoon neutral oil or melted ghee,
   plus more for kneading and brushing

½ cup water

☙ INGREDIENT NOTE

You can use any whole wheat flour, but atta, Indian whole wheat flour, works the best. It's not too high in protein, so it results in soft and very pliable parathas.

❄ FREEZER NOTE

You can freeze cooked parathas in an airtight container or ziplock bag for up to 2 months. Freeze them in a stack, each one separated by a sheet of parchment paper so they don't stick to one another. To reheat, just put a paratha directly from the freezer into a skillet and cook over low heat until heated through. Or store at room temp for up to 2 days or in the fridge for up to a week.

The variety of Indian flatbreads could (and probably should) have its own multiseason Netflix show. It's a vast and delicious world, and there are even several types of parathas made from a variety of flours and ranging in degrees of flakiness. These basic ones are made from whole wheat flour and don't have many layers (see the recipe for Super Flaky Parathas on page 247 if you're looking for that!), but they are very tender and pair well with many dishes, from Rajma (page 191) to Paneer Tikka Masala (page 185), and serve as a base for Hash Brown, Egg, and Cheese Kati Rolls (page 101).

In a large bowl, combine the flour, salt, cumin seeds, and oil and mix well. Add the water to the flour mixture a few tablespoons at a time, mixing by hand (or with a wooden spoon) until a dough forms. Knead by hand for about 2 minutes, until the dough becomes smooth and taut. Add some oil to your hands and continue to knead for another minute or so. At this point, the dough should be a bit tacky but should not stick to your fingers. If you press your thumb into the dough, it should leave an imprint. Pinch the dough off into 1½-inch balls. You should have 10 to 12 balls. On a lightly floured surface, roll out each dough ball into a 5-inch circle.

Heat a large skillet over medium heat. Add 1 paratha and cook for about 30 seconds, until bubbles form on top, then flip the paratha. Brush the side facing up with a little bit of oil and cook for 30 seconds. Flip the paratha again, brush the other side with oil, and cook for 15 seconds. Transfer to a paper towel–lined plate and cover with a kitchen towel to keep warm. Continue to cook all the parathas in the same way. Feel free to stack them as you go.

Super Flaky Parathas

1 cup all-purpose flour, plus
more for dusting

½ teaspoon sugar

½ teaspoon salt

¼ teaspoon baking powder

1½ teaspoons neutral oil, plus
more for brushing

⅓ cup water

Flakier parathas take more patience than Simple Parathas (page 244) but are worth the effort. Made from all-purpose flour and a good amount of oil, these are more like the crois-sants of the Indian flatbread universe: wonderfully flaky thanks to thin layers and the generous use of fat. Rolling the dough into a spiral and then flattening it into a disk creates layers without an entire lamination process.

Serve these parathas with a pot of Chana Masala (page 197) or Classic Butter Chicken (page 188). Or eat them as I would: spread with mashed avocado and topped with scrambled eggs, feta cheese, and hot sauce. If you have any leftovers, transform them into a plate of Egg and Vegetable Kottu Parotta (page 37).

In a medium bowl, combine the flour, sugar, salt, baking powder, oil, and water. Using your hands or a wooden spoon, bring the mixture together into a soft dough that is not crumbly. Knead the dough for 5 minutes, then cover it and set aside for 2 hours or so to let the gluten in the dough rest.

Divide the dough into 6 balls and let rest for at least 10 minutes before you start to roll them out. Roll out 1 dough ball into a disk about 3 inches in diameter. Brush with oil and place on a plate. Repeat with the remaining dough balls, brushing each disk with oil and stacking the disks on top of one another. Let rest for 20 minutes.

Recipe continues

On a lightly floured surface, roll out 1 disk into a thin circle about 6 inches in diameter. The dough should spread very, very easily at this point. Roll up the circle into a thin tube and then curl the tube into a spiral. Repeat with the remaining dough disks. Rest the spirals for about 5 minutes, then roll each one back out into a 6- to 7-inch circle.

Heat a nonstick skillet over medium-low heat. Place 1 paratha in the pan, cook for 1 minute, and then flip it. Brush the cooked side with a little bit of oil, cook for 1 minute, and flip it back over. Brush the other side with a little bit of oil and cook until the paratha is cooked through and golden, 1 to 2 minutes. Transfer to a paper towel–lined plate and cover with a kitchen towel to keep warm. Continue to cook all the parathas in the same way. To make them extra flaky, stack the cooked parathas and gently squish together the edges of the parathas.

Masala Thepla

2 cups whole wheat flour (atta)

4 ½ teaspoons neutral oil, divided,
   plus more for cooking

1 ½ teaspoons salt

1 teaspoon ground turmeric

½ teaspoon cumin seeds

½ teaspoon ajwain seeds
   (carom seeds; optional)

½ teaspoon Kashmiri red chili powder

2 tablespoons plain yogurt
   (see Ingredient Note)

¾ cup water

All-purpose flour, for dusting

🌿 INGREDIENT NOTE

The thicker the yogurt used, the more water will be needed, so if you're using Greek yogurt, you will need a few more tablespoons of water to achieve the right consistency. I prefer to use full-fat yogurt.

There is no trip in my family without thepla. It doesn't matter if it is a 5-hour car ride to my uncle's house or a 16-hour plane journey to India, you could always bank on my mom packing a stack of thepla for the road. Even now that I am an adult, my mom offers to make me a pile of the Indian flatbreads for my flight home.

My family is not alone in this. Look around the parking lot of any national park or theme park, and you're guaranteed to find a Gujarati American family, with the trunk of their car open, snacking from a steel container of thepla, alongside fresh fruit and whatever snacks they could cram into a cooler.

Part of it comes from a place of frugality—thepla are inexpensive to make—but it's also because they are simply the perfect travel food. These flatbreads remain tender and pliable at room temperature for days, thanks to the addition of yogurt to the dough. Thepla are great rolled up on their own, and they are relatively nutritious, especially when compared to concession stand pizza or lukewarm airline meals. When I'm not traveling, I like to eat them with a bowl of plain yogurt or a spoonful of mango pickle.

Recipe continues

Cooked thepla freeze well in an air-tight container or ziplock bag for up to 2 months. They are easy to reheat on the stovetop or in the microwave, covered with a damp paper towel to keep them from drying out. Or store at room temp for up to 3 days or in the fridge for up to a week.

Sift the flour into a large bowl. Add 4 teaspoons oil, the salt, turmeric, cumin seeds, ajwain (if using), and chili powder. Mix with your hands until evenly combined. (You could use a spoon, but I swear the thepla tastes better when mixed by hand.) Add the yogurt and mix with your hands until gently combined. Sprinkle about ¼ cup water over the mixture and form a loose dough. Continue to add the rest of the water, bit by bit, until the dough achieves a smooth consistency. The dough should be soft, but not very sticky. Think: the texture of Play-Doh. Pour the remaining ½ teaspoon oil over the dough and knead by hand for a minute. Pinch off 2-tablespoon clumps of dough and roll into 1-inch balls. You should have 16 to 20 balls. Gently dust each dough ball with all-purpose flour. On a lightly floured surface, flatten each dough ball and then roll out into a thin circle, about 6 inches in diameter and ½ inch thick.

Heat a large skillet over medium heat. Place one circle in the pan. Once it starts bubbling, flip it over and brush a little bit of oil on the cooked side, making sure the surface is covered. Cook for 15 seconds, then transfer to a plate lined with paper towels and cover with a kitchen towel to keep warm. Continue to cook all the thepla in the same way, stacking them on the plate.

Puri

2 cups whole wheat flour (atta),
   plus more for dusting

1 teaspoon salt

4 teaspoons neutral oil, plus
   more for frying

½ cup water, plus more if needed

🌿 INGREDIENT NOTE

It is best to use atta, or whole wheat flour, from the Indian store for the best texture. If you use a brand like King Arthur flour, it might be higher in protein and will require more water to bring the dough together, resulting in a heavier and tougher puri.

❄ FREEZER NOTE

You can freeze extra puri dough in an airtight container for up to 3 months. Thaw in the fridge before rolling and frying. Do not freeze cooked puri.

When I was growing up, my friend Yasi would get so excited whenever my mom would fry up a fresh batch of puri that she would do what we called her "puri dance." It's easy to see why she was obsessed: puffy, golden puri pulled piping-hot out of the oil is a god-tier food moment I hope everyone experiences at least once (ideally several times) in their lives.

Given that they are deep-fried, puri—which are beloved across the Indian subcontinent—were always a special-occasion food that my mom would save for birthday dinners, anniversaries, Diwali parties, and large gatherings. If I came into the kitchen and there was Shrikhand (page 291), Chana Masala (page 197), and puri on the counter, I knew someone important was coming over or a celebration was about to happen.

There are two keys to making perfect puri. One, roll out only a few puri at a time before frying them. If you try to roll them all out ahead of time, the dough will seize up and the puri will not fry evenly. Two, rapidly tap each puri with a slotted spoon so that it submerges under the oil as soon as it goes in. This will help the puri properly puff. Fully cooked puri will eventually deflate after a few minutes, but that is okay because they are ridiculously good.

Recipe continues

In a medium bowl, mix the flour, salt, and oil together by hand. The dough will be crumbly. Pour the water into the bowl in batches, and knead the dough for about 2 minutes, until the dough becomes smooth and is not sticky to the touch. You don't want to overwork the dough!

On a lightly floured surface, divide the dough into about 24 balls about 1 inch in diameter, place on a plate, and cover with a clean kitchen towel until you are ready to fry.

In your favorite frying vessel, heat 3 to 4 inches of oil until it hits 375 degrees F.

On a clean, dry surface, roll 1 dough ball at a time into a 3-inch circle and carefully drop it into the hot oil. Using a slotted spoon or a spider, tap the dough a couple of times to quickly submerge the puri in the oil. This will help it fully puff. After 10 seconds or so the puri should be golden brown on one side; flip the puri and cook until the other side is also golden brown, 15 to 20 seconds. Place the puri on a plate lined with paper towels. Repeat until you have fried all the puri.

Simple Naan

2 cups all-purpose flour, plus
more for dusting

1 teaspoon sugar

1 teaspoon salt

1 teaspoon baking powder

¼ teaspoon baking soda

4 teaspoons neutral oil, plus
more for greasing

¼ cup plain full-fat Greek yogurt

¼ cup water, plus more if needed

2 teaspoons kalonji (nigella
seeds; optional)

Melted butter, for topping

EXTRA CREDIT
Use the naan as a base for pizza, and you can
find more ideas on page 149.

I wish I had the setup to make epic restaurant-style naan. You know, the kind that arrive at the table impossibly soft and bubbly, dripping with butter, after being cooked against the side of a searing-hot tandoor. I hope there is a personal clay oven in my future, but until that day comes, I will stick to this recipe for a truly simple naan (that doesn't require any kind of oven at all).

Naan is one the few Indian breads that is often made with yeast, but as someone who frequently forgets to leave enough time for a dough to proof before I need to use it, I wanted to create a recipe using more instant leaveners. This dough still needs at least an hour to rest before you can shape and roll out the naan, but after that it comes together quickly.

The coolest part of this recipe is a trick I picked up on TikTok (shoutout to hours of doomscrolling finally being useful!), where if you fling a little water onto the hot pan before cooking the dough, you can create blistery bubbles on your naan. If you want garlic naan, add minced garlic and minced fresh cilantro to the butter before brushing it on the bread.

In a large bowl, combine the flour, sugar, salt, baking powder, and baking soda and mix well with a wooden spoon. (You can also use a stand mixer with a dough hook, and mix the ingredients on low.) Mix in the oil and yogurt. Add the water and start kneading the dough either with your hands or with the dough hook on low speed, scraping down the sides of the bowl at regular intervals. You want to knead for 2 to 3 minutes, a few minutes longer if kneading by hand, until the dough is soft and stretchy but not sticky. If you need to add more water to the dough to achieve this texture, do so a teaspoon at a time. (Take care not to add too much water to the dough.) Shape the dough into a ball, place in a lightly oiled bowl, cover, and let rest in a warm spot for at least 1 hour.

Transfer the dough to a lightly floured work surface. Use a chef's knife or a sharp bench scraper to cut the dough into 8 parts. Roll each part into a smooth dough ball between your palms. Roll out each dough ball into an oval shape that is about 8 inches long. If you're using the kalonji, spread them across the dough and then use the rolling pin to press them into the dough.

Heat a large nonstick skillet over medium-high heat. Use your fingers or a pastry brush to fling water droplets all over the pan (this is how you'll get the bubbly blistered naan effect without needing a tandoor oven). Place 1 naan, nigella side up, in the pan and cook for 1 to 1½ minutes. Large bubbles will start to form. Flip the naan and cook on the other side for another minute or so. Remove the naan from the pan and brush with a generous amount of melted butter. Repeat the process with the remaining dough, and stack the finished naan on a plate, covered with a clean towel to keep in the heat.

Tadka Focaccia

2 ½ cups lukewarm water

1 (¼-ounce) envelope active dry
   yeast (2 ¼ teaspoons)

2 teaspoons honey

5 cups all-purpose flour

1 tablespoon ground turmeric

1 tablespoon salt

6 ½ tablespoons olive oil

Butter, for greasing

¼ cup ghee, unsalted butter,
   or additional olive oil

2 teaspoons black mustard seeds

4 teaspoons white sesame seeds

4 or 5 dried red chiles

20 to 30 fresh curry leaves

Flaky sea salt

When I want fresh bread, I make focaccia. It's a very forgiving dough and can be made from start to finish in one day if you start early enough. I am always in awe of the beautiful Indian-inspired sourdough boules my friend Kusuma Rao makes on Instagram, with ingredients like polenta, turmeric, pepitas, and a mustard seed and curry leaf tadka baked right in. It inspired me to dream up this tadka-topped focaccia loaded with crispy curry leaves, black mustard seeds, white sesame seeds, and dried red chiles. The turmeric in the dough doesn't add much flavor, but I love the hue it imparts to the final product.

I like my focaccia thick, so I bake it in a 9 x 13–inch pan, but use a rimmed baking sheet if you like yours thinner. I keep it thick so I can slice it in half to make sandwiches. The bread pairs well with Spicy Cilantro Chutney Mussels (page 218) and Indian Tomato Soup (page 238).

In a medium bowl, whisk together the lukewarm water, yeast, and honey and let it sit for about 5 minutes. After that it should start to look foamy; if it doesn't, then it's likely your yeast is dead and you need to get fresh yeast and start over! To the yeast mixture, add the flour, turmeric, and salt and mix with a silicone spatula or your hands until a shaggy dough forms.

Pour 4 tablespoons olive oil into a very large bowl (that can fit in your fridge), add the dough, and move the dough around so that it is coated in the oil. Cover the bowl with plastic wrap or a towel and let it rise in the fridge for at least 8 hours or up to one day. You can also let it rise at room temperature for 3 to 4 hours. The dough should look quite bubbly and have doubled in size.

Recipe continues

Using two forks or spoons, gather the edges of the dough farthest away from you in the bowl and lift that edge over toward the center of the dough. Give the bowl a quarter-turn and repeat until all four sides have been folded toward the center. Then repeat this process 3 more times. Pour in 1 tablespoon olive oil and make sure all of the dough is coated. Let it rise, uncovered, in a warm, dry spot for at least 1½ hours. It should double in size again. It's ready if you press on the dough with a finger and it slowly springs back.

Preheat the oven to 450 degrees F. Butter a 9 x 13–inch baking dish and pour 1 tablespoon olive oil into the center of the pan. Pour the dough into the pan, stretching it to make sure it touches the edges, and with lightly oiled hands, dimple the focaccia all over. Think of it as putty or Play-Doh and really press down so that you can feel the bottom of the pan.

Melt the ghee in a small, heavy-bottomed saucepan. Add the mustard seeds and let them pop for 10 seconds, then remove the pan from the heat, add the sesame seeds, red chiles, and curry leaves, and cover the pan for a minute. Swirl the mixture, then evenly brush it onto the dimpled dough. Drizzle the dough with the remaining ½ tablespoon oil and sprinkle with flaky sea salt. Bake for 25 minutes, or until the top is golden and the bread feels puffy. Cut the focaccia into squares.

Masala Roasted Garlic Bread

4 heads garlic

4 teaspoons olive oil

2 tablespoons ghee, at room temperature

Handful finely chopped fresh cilantro

2 teaspoons Chaat Masala (page 63)

1 crusty baguette

❄ FREEZER NOTE

To freeze, prepare the garlic bread up until the step of cutting and baking it. Wrap the baguette tightly in plastic wrap, then in aluminum foil. Freeze for up to 3 months. To eat, bake the loaf as you normally would, though it might need a few additional minutes.

One afternoon, I was prepping for a dinner party and my menu felt like it was missing something. The lineup centered around a tray of Saag Paneer Lasagna (page 169), paired with an Endive and Paneer Salad (page 234), and then a Mango Pie (page 282) firming up in the fridge for dessert. I needed one more easy side, but I didn't have time to hit the store. I spied a baguette I had picked up the day before, and an Indian-inspired garlic bread was the answer I was searching for.

Four whole heads of garlic might seem like a lot, but roasting garlic mellows out the flavor and gives it a wonderfully buttery texture.

Preheat the oven to 400 degrees F.

Slice ¼ to ½ inch off the top of each head of garlic so that the tips of the cloves are exposed. Place the heads on a piece of aluminum foil in a small baking dish. Pour the olive oil all over the garlic and wrap the foil so that that garlic is enclosed. Roast for 55 to 60 minutes, until the garlic is soft. Leave the oven on. Open the foil and let the garlic cool a bit, then squeeze the cloves out of their skins directly into a medium bowl. Add the ghee, cilantro, and chaat masala. Stir well to combine.

Line a rimmed baking sheet with parchment paper. Cut the baguette into quarters, then slice each quarter in half horizontally so you have 8 pieces. Spread each piece with a generous layer of the garlicky ghee mixture. Place the bread on the prepared baking sheet and bake for 10 minutes, or until the bread is toasted. Move the baking sheet up to the top rack, turn the oven to broil, and broil for 2 minutes, or until the garlic bread is perfectly crunchy and brown.

10 THINGS YOU NEED TO KNOW

1 As with meat (see page 92), Indians both in India and in the diaspora have a complicated relationship with alcohol. (Sorry; we make nothing easy.) A lot of this is due to religious reasons, but some of it is cultural, too. (The western Indian state of Gujarat is legally a dry state, meaning no alcohol is allowed to be consumed or sold.) Only one-third of India's population regularly consumes alcohol, and most of those people are men.

2 This is not to say that Indians don't enjoy drinking. Just look at pop culture. There's plenty of legendary Bollywood and Punjabi songs dedicated to the joys of drinking or being drunk. I could make you a very robust playlist.

3 Unlike, say, Korea with soju, Mexico with tequila, and Peru with pisco, India doesn't have a well-known home-grown alcoholic product. There is feni, a distilled liquor made with cashew fruit or toddy palm from coconut trees; palm wine, which comes from fermenting the sap of palm trees; and apo, a fermented rice alcohol—but nothing mainstream or easy to purchase.

4 India doesn't have a strong wine culture, though this is starting to change as more South Asians are making wine in places like California and Seattle. This doesn't mean that Indian food doesn't pair well with wine, though. If you don't want to think about it too hard, all Indian food goes especially well with a cold bottle of champagne (that is my favorite dinner party trick).

5 What Indians do love to drink is whiskey. One, because it is high in alcohol content, so a little bit goes a long way, and two, because whiskey was often correlated with wealth and the upper class, especially during the days of colonialism. There are a number of homegrown whiskey brands now, but nothing will ever beat the obsession Indians have with Johnnie Walker. Go to any wedding, any party, any restaurant, and if there is a bottle of whiskey, it will be Johnnie Walker. The whiskey is so popular among Indians that actor Badruddin Jamaluddin Kazi even changed his screen name to Johnny Walker, after once playing the role of a drunk.

6 Beer is almost as popular as whiskey. Kingfisher is India's best-selling beer and is easily found globally. And beer happens to pair really well with Indian food.

7 The Indian obsession with chai is common knowledge at this point, though the regional varieties and differences are not as well known (like noon chai, which hails from Kashmir in the north and has a distinct pink hue and sweet flavor).

8 Many people are surprised to learn that India also has a robust coffee culture. There are several coffee farms, especially in south India. And a proper cup of south Indian filter coffee, also known as filter kaapi, is one of the best ways to consume coffee. Strong coffee is brewed, combined with milk and sugar, and then aerated by pouring the liquid between two cups, ideally from a tall height, so that the coffee gets extra frothy.

9 The Indian nonalcoholic drink options are fun, creative, and refreshing. They range from savory, like spiced buttermilk (known as masala chaas); to sweet, like lassi; to tart, like aam panna, a drink made from green mangoes. One of my favorite drinks is Badam Doodh (page 266), which is milk flavored with almonds and saffron.

10 Indian sodas, or "cold drinks," are some of the most delicious in the world if you love carbonation. Thums Up, an Indian cola, and Limca, which has a sharp lemon-lime flavor, are available at most Indian grocery store. Like all sodas, they are best when enjoyed out of a glass bottle.

DRINI

Indians in the diaspora are a big beverage culture. No guest will ever be offered just water—even if it is 11 p.m. There will always be an offer to make chai, or coffee, one of several nonalcoholic options like falooda (though one could argue that is borderline a dessert), or, if you're lucky, a cocktail—or three.

Badam Doodh

1 tablespoon water

2 ½ cups whole milk

2 tablespoons sugar

½ teaspoon saffron threads

3 tablespoons blanched sliced almonds

1 tablespoon crushed pistachios

1 teaspoon ground cardamom

 **INGREDIENT NOTE**

If you don't drink dairy, oat or soy milk also works well.

STORAGE NOTE

You cannot freeze badam doodh, but it stays well in an airtight container in the fridge for up to 5 days.

Badam doodh means "almond milk," but it is not milk made from almonds. Instead, it is milk—the kind from cows—with almonds in it. During the harsh Michigan winters when I was growing up, my mom would often make a hot version of this nutty but sweet drink. When I was 5, I burned my tongue at an ice skating rink drinking hot chocolate made from a packet and scalding hot water, and it put me off hot chocolate for life. Badam doodh, on the other hand, has never injured me and remains one of my favorite cold weather drinks. In the summer, badam doodh is perfect over ice.

Heat a small, heavy-bottomed saucepan over medium heat. Pour in the water and let it quickly warm up, about 15 seconds (this helps the milk to not stick). Then add the milk and bring to a gentle simmer.

While the milk is simmering, in a small bowl, microwave the saffron strands for 15 seconds—this helps dry it out. Crumble the saffron between your fingers until it is a powder. This method lets you use less saffron but still get the same beautiful color and flavor. Add the saffron to the milk and stir. Add the almonds, pistachios, and cardamom. Turn the heat up to high and let the milk boil for about 3 minutes, until it starts to slightly thicken. Serve hot or cold over ice.

Cold Coffee
with Ice Cream

2 cups cold whole milk (you can use another milk, even plant-based, but some fat makes it taste better)

3 tablespoons sugar

4 teaspoons instant coffee, preferably Nescafé

8 to 12 ice cubes

4 scoops high-quality vanilla ice cream

❄ FREEZER NOTE
Do not freeze. Consume immediately.

Before Starbucks cornered the frozen coffee drink market with the Frappuccino, there was cold coffee with ice cream. It's also known as a coffee milkshake, but it's much thinner in texture than what we consider to be a milkshake in America. This drink is brilliant in its simplicity, thanks to instant coffee. And no, I will not tolerate any instant coffee slander. It's a truly incredible invention, and how so many Indians make their coffee. If you can only stomach single-origin, hand-roasted pour-over coffee, this is not for you. Don't skimp on the quality of the vanilla ice cream, though: this recipe is where you splurge for the good stuff.

Put the milk, sugar, and instant coffee in a blender and blend until frothy, about 30 seconds. Divide the ice cubes between 4 glasses, then pour about ½ cup of the blended coffee into each. Gently plop a scoop of ice cream into each glass and serve with a spoon.

VANILLA ICE CREAM

ROSE MILK

BASIL SEEDS

ROSE JELLY

VERMICELLI

BOBA

Bobalooda

SEEDS

2 teaspoons basil or chia seeds

2 tablespoons cold water

ROSE JELLY

3 tablespoons rose syrup,
  such as Rooh Afza

2 teaspoons agar-agar

1½ cups cold water

VERMICELLI

½ ounce rice vermicelli

MILK BASE

1½ cups cold milk (you can use
  oat or soy milk if you want)

3 tablespoons rose syrup

½ cup boba pearls, cooked according
  to package instructions

1 cup vanilla ice cream

Chopped pistachios and dried edible
  rose petals, for garnish (optional)

Falooda is not quite a drink, not quite a dessert, but it is a textural wonderland. The slippery crunch of jelled basil seeds (or chia seeds), the bite of slithery rice vermicelli noodles, the jiggle from cubes of rose jelly, all swimming in a creamy base of rose syrup and milk, and topped with a scoop of ice cream.

This might sound like *a lot* already, but as a texture fiend I think falooda is always missing one thing: a super chewy element. The solution? Boba, aka tapioca pearls, the foundation of bubble tea. You can easily find instant boba pearls at any Asian market or even stores like Trader Joe's. If you want to add other bubble tea toppings, like nata de coco pieces or lychee jelly, to your bobalooda, I won't stop you.

In a small bowl, stir together the basil seeds and water. Cover and let soak in the fridge for at least 20 minutes or as long as 12 hours so that the seeds plump up and bloom. Set aside.

To make the rose jelly, in a small saucepan, whisk together the rose syrup, agar-agar, and cold water until well combined. Bring the mixture to a boil over high heat and cook for 1 minute, whisking constantly. Immediately pour the mixture into a loaf pan and let cool undisturbed at room temperature. It will take about 45 minutes to set. Once it feels set but jiggly, run a knife around the edge of the pan and flip the jelly over onto a cutting board. Cut the jelly into ½-inch cubes and set aside.

While the jelly is setting, cook the rice vermicelli according to the package instructions. Drain the noodles and rinse under cold water.

Recipe continues

Traditionally, falooda is made with basil seeds, also known as tukmaria or sabja. They are readily available at any Indian grocery store, but I often swap them out for chia seeds, which I always have on hand.

Don't freeze the falooda.

Just before you are ready to serve, make the milk base by whisking together the cold milk and rose syrup in something that is easy to pour out of.

Divide the cooked boba pearls between 2 tall glasses (at least 12 ounces). Add 2 tablespoons vermicelli to each glass. Top that layer with about ½ cup rose jelly cubes (feel free to use less if you prefer). Carefully pour ¾ cup milk base into each glass, and top each with 1 tablespoon bloomed basil seeds. Scoop ½ cup vanilla ice cream onto the top layer in each glass, and garnish with pistachios and rose petals, if using. Serve with a boba straw or spoon, or both.

Pani Puri Mojito

PANI PURI CONCENTRATE

Handful fresh cilantro

Handful fresh mint

½ green serrano pepper

½-inch piece fresh ginger

1 teaspoon cumin seeds

1 teaspoon Chaat Masala (page 63)

½ teaspoon salt

Juice of 1 lime

¼ cup water

MOJITO

1 tablespoon sugar

6 to 8 fresh mint leaves

Juice of 1 lime, plus lime wheels
    for garnish (optional)

2 ounces white rum

4 ounces cold club soda

❧ INGREDIENT NOTE

For this recipe, I ask you to make a very concentrated version of the pani, to help simplify the process. It's important to run the pani puri concentrate through a sieve before adding it to the cocktail or the drink will have clumps.

❄ FREEZER NOTE

You can freeze the concentrate in an airtight container for up to 2 months. Thaw in the fridge before using.

One of my more rebellious moments as a teenager was zipping around my parents hometown of Ahmedabad, India, eating all the glorious late night street food with my cousin Sagar. Due to concerns over the unfiltered water, I was specifically told to not eat the streetside pani puri—so of course I ate the streetside pani puri.

It's a snack that is meant to be eaten one at a time, made to order. The vendor would crack a hole in the puri, a delicate little fried sphere made from semolina, and stuff it with spiced potatoes and lentils, before topping it with tamarind chutney and dunking it in the pani, or water. Pani, when made right, tends to look like pond water but tastes incredibly fresh and herbaceous thanks to the generous use of cilantro, mint, and ginger. The idea is to eat the dunked puri in a single bite. And repeat until you physically cannot eat another bite.

I've seen a lot of restaurants in the diaspora add tequila to the pani for their pani puri (a dish that is also often called gol gappe). I never understood the move, because pani puri is perfect as is. But they're onto something with combining alcohol and pani. Taking that herbaceous minty water, muddling it with sugar, and adding lime and rum really does transform the pani into an incredibly refreshing cocktail.

Combine all of the ingredients for the pani puri concentrate in a blender and blend until smooth. It should have the consistency of a watery smoothie or pesto.

Pour 1 ounce of the pani puri concentrate through a fine-mesh sieve into a tall glass. Add the sugar and mint and muddle the mixture. Pour in the lime juice, rum, and club soda. Give it a good stir to combine. Top with ice and garnish with a lime wheel or two, if you like.

Tamarind Chutney Margarita

Juice of 1 lime, plus 2 lime wedges

Sugar, for the rim

2 ounces reposado tequila

½ ounce Cointreau

1 ounce Tamarind Chutney (page 52)

❄ FREEZER NOTE

I wouldn't freeze the margarita, but to make it a frozen margarita, combine all of the ingredients in a blender with some ice.

Tamarind and tequila are best friends, and a tamarind margarita is proof of that. And tamarind chutney—which is already sweetened and spiced with a little cumin and chili powder—is a better base than just plain tamarind. Having the chutney on hand makes this cocktail a breeze to whip up: you add the ingredients to a shaker with ice and strain. It's also very easy to scale up the recipe for a crowd. These margaritas are especially fun to drink with a tray of Rajma Nachos (page 174) and a stack of Aloo Paratha Quesadillas (page 177). This is very easy to batch for a big group!

Squeeze the juice from 1 lime wedge around the rim of a glass. Pour some sugar onto a plate, then dip the rim of the glass into the sugar.

Combine the tequila, Cointreau, tamarind chutney, and lime juice in a shaker with ice. Shake until cold. Fill the sugar-rimmed glass with ice and then strain the drink through a sieve into the glass. Garnish with the remaining lime wedge.

PANI PURI MOJITO

SHIKANJI PIMM'S CUP

SAFFRON GIN
AND TONIC

The Indian canon of sweets is such a dramatic departure from what Americans and Europeans expect dessert to be. While the West relies upon flour, eggs, and leaveners, the building blocks of Indian sweet-making include the generous use of nuts, jaggery (an unrefined cane sugar rich in flavor), lots of ghee, and slow-cooked milk (known as khoya). Therefore, Indian desserts tend to be denser and sweeter. Each bite packs a real punch. "Not too sweet," is a nonexistent descriptor. When it comes to Indian desserts, the sweeter the better.

DESS

ERTS

Mango Pie

GRAHAM CRACKER CRUST

3 cups finely ground graham cracker
   crumbs (about 24 sheets)

½ cup sugar

½ teaspoon ground black cardamom

Pinch salt

12 tablespoons (1½ sticks)
   unsalted butter, melted

FILLING

½ cup cold water

2 (¾-ounce) envelopes unflavored gelatin

1 (30-ounce) can mango pulp

1 (8-ounce) block full-fat cream
   cheese, at room temperature

½ cup condensed milk

Whipped cream for topping (optional)

I am convinced there is an auntie whisper network that you were initiated into if you immigrated to the United States from India between 1970 and 1990. There are certain set recipes they all seem to know, no matter where they live, that cleverly blend American grocery store staples with Indian flavors (see Breakfast Cereal Chevvdo, page 74, and Easy Freezer Kulfi, page 290). Perhaps the best of them all is this jiggly mango pie.

The key to the pie is canned mango pulp, which is easily found at Indian stores or online groceries. (Fresh mango puree would likely work, but you would need to add a decent amount of sugar.) It's blended with cream cheese and gelatin to create a creamy filling with satisfying bounce. Many aunties I know would use a premade store-bought graham cracker crust, but I prefer to make my own crust with a pinch of salt and ground cardamom. This takes the pie to a new level. When making this for a party, I like to use a 9 x 13-inch baking pan and then cut the pie into squares for easy serving.

Preheat the oven to 350 degrees F.

To make the crust, combine the graham cracker crumbs, sugar, cardamom, and salt in a medium bowl and stir to evenly combine. Pour in the melted butter and mix again so that the butter is evenly distributed and the mixture starts to clump together. If you're making 2 pies, divide the mixture between 2 (9-inch) pie pans and use your fingers to press down on the mixture to create an even and compact crust that runs up the sides of the pans. If you're making 1 large pie, line a 9 x 13-inch baking pan with parchment paper so that it overhangs the sides of the pan (this will make it easier to serve), then press the crumbs into an even layer across the bottom of the pan.

Recipe continues

Bake for 10 to 12 minutes (you might need a few more minutes if using the 9 x 13 pan). The crust should be golden brown but not too dark—like it spent time in the sun but wore lots of sunscreen. Let cool completely.

To make the filling, pour the cold water into a saucepan and sprinkle the 2 gelatin packets over the water. Let it sit for 5 minutes, then place the saucepan over medium heat and stir until the gelatin is fully dissolved. Let the mixture cool. Transfer the gelatin mixture to a blender, along with the mango pulp, cream cheese, and condensed milk. Blitz until well combined and there are no cream cheese chunks.

Divide the mango mixture between the pie crusts or pour into the 9 x 13 pan and use a silicone spatula to make sure the filling is even and smooth. Cover and refrigerate for at least 4 hours until firm. (I prefer to refrigerate it overnight.) Serve chilled, garnished with whipped cream, if you so desire.

Gulab Jamun

CHASNI (SYRUP)

20 to 25 saffron threads

3½ cups sugar

3 cups water

1 tablespoon rose water

JAMUN

Neutral oil, for frying

2 cups dry milk powder

1 cup Bisquick

1 teaspoon ground cardamom

2 cups heavy cream

I have yet to meet a person who can resist the power of a gulab jamun, arguably the most popular Indian dessert in America. It's rare to come across an Indian restaurant that doesn't have gulab jamun on the dessert menu and/or any wedding that isn't serving them to guests.

In India, the saffron syrup–soaked doughnuts are traditionally made with khoya, which is milk that has been boiled down for hours. It is possible to find khoya these days at Indian stores across the country, but that is a more recent development. Resourceful Indian Americans have made gulab jamun for decades with a surprising ingredient: Bisquick.

Combined with dried milk powder, Bisquick results in a texture that I'd argue is even better than the traditional version. Just make sure to fry the gulab jamun low and slow. If the oil is too hot, the jamun will brown too fast and taste slightly burnt. Gulab jamun are ridiculously good cold out of the fridge, at room temperature, or after being warmed up in the microwave for 30 seconds.

It's important to make the chasni, or syrup, first so it has a chance to cool down before dropping in the jamun to soak. In a small bowl, microwave the saffron for 25 seconds. This will dry it out to make it easier to break up the threads. Combine the sugar and water in a medium saucepan over medium heat and stir until the sugar dissolves. Crush the saffron between your fingers and add it to the pan. Turn the heat up to high and bring the mixture to a boil. Boil for 2 minutes, then remove the pan from the heat and add the rose water. Set the syrup aside to cool to room temperature.

Recipe continues

While the syrup cools, make the jamun. In your favorite deep frying vessel, heat 3 to 4 inches oil until it hits 350 degrees F.

In a medium bowl, mix the milk powder, Bisquick, and cardamom until evenly combined. Add the cream and bring the dough together with a spoon or with your hands until it forms a smooth, soft ball that doesn't crack. (If the dough feels dry, you can add water, a teaspoon at a time, until it reaches the desired consistency.) The dough should be soft, but it shouldn't stick to your hands. If it does stick, add a little more milk powder. Pinch off 1-inch balls of dough and roll between your palms until smooth. Set aside on a plate and cover with a kitchen towel. You should have 36 to 40 balls.

Drop 3 or 4 dough balls into the hot oil. Bubbles should form around the dough as soon as you drop them in. Using a slotted spoon, keep turning the jamun until they are evenly brown and golden on all sides, 2 to 3 minutes. If they brown faster than that, you need to drop the temperature of your oil. Using a slotted spoon, transfer the jamun to a plate lined with paper towels. Repeat until all the jamun are fried. Once they are slightly cooled, add the jamun to the syrup mixture. Make sure each jamun is submerged in the syrup. Let soak for 4 to 6 hours at room temperature before serving.

Indian Fruit Salad

CUSTARD

4 cups whole milk

2 tablespoons custard powder
(see Ingredient Note)

6 tablespoons sugar, divided

1 teaspoon ground cardamom

FRUIT

2 or 3 bananas, diced

1 medium apple, peeled if
desired, cored, and diced

1 (8-ounce) can mandarin
oranges, drained

1 (4-ounce) can pineapple chunks, drained

¾ cup diced grapes

 **INGREDIENT NOTE**

Custard powder adds flavor and helps thicken the milk. It's readily available at most grocery stores (I use Bird's brand). If you cannot find custard powder, an equal amount of vanilla instant pudding mix should work (but I haven't ever made it this way).

❄ **FREEZER NOTE**

You can freeze the custard base without the fruit in an airtight container for months.

This is not fruit salad, but *froot suh-laahd.* (It's how every auntie pronounces it, so therefore it is canon.) This recipe is a far cry from a pile of chopped mixed fruit garnished with a few sprigs of mint and perhaps a drizzle of honey. In *froot suh-laahd*, the fruit pieces are swimming in a pool of super cold custard-flavored milk. It's a staple of dinner parties in many Indian American households because it feeds a crowd with ease, is incredibly easy to put together, and nails being sweet but refreshing at the same time.

This recipe utilizes a mix of canned and fresh fruit, but feel free to customize your fruit blend. The addition of pomegranate arils and fresh mango chunks would be delicious, as would nuts like cashews. I am a texture fiend and believe a chewy or jelly element, such as boba or nata de coco, would work well, too. There is only one real rule: canned pineapple is fine, but fresh pineapple is not—unless you enjoy curdled milk.

In a small, heavy-bottomed saucepan, heat the milk over medium heat. In a small bowl, whisk together the custard powder, 2 tablespoons sugar, and ½ cup warm milk from the pan. There should be no clumps. Once the milk starts boiling, stir in the custard mixture, then mix in the remaining 4 tablespoons sugar and let boil for 5 minutes so that the flavors meld and the custard powder cooks. Remove the pan from the heat and stir in the cardamom. Cool to room temperature, then cover and refrigerate overnight. Add the fruit to the milk mixture. Pour into a large, fun bowl if having a party.

Easy Freezer Kulfi

1 (14-ounce) can condensed milk

1 (12-ounce) can evaporated milk

1½ cups heavy cream or Cool Whip

1 cup skinless almonds

1½ teaspoons ground cardamom, divided

2 pinches saffron

¼ cup chopped pistachios

❋ **FREEZER NOTE**

If it isn't obvious, this kulfi should be frozen!

There was a good decade when I was growing up that every auntie I knew served up some version of this decadent but truly simple kulfi, straight from their freezer. Made with supermarket basics, it's basically a rite of passage for Indian aunties to learn to make this when they immigrate to America.

Kulfi is often explained as "Indian ice cream," but that isn't quite accurate. Yes, it's a creamy, dairy-based frozen dessert, but it requires none of the churning, is much denser in texture, and is nearly impossible to scoop. Traditionally made from milk that is boiled down for hours until super thick, it is often frozen in molds and served on a stick or sold by the slice. You can find kulfi in all kinds of flavors—mango, strawberry, pistachio, chocolate—but my favorite will always be kesar pista, aka saffron pistachio. This more "instant" version uses a mix of condensed milk, evaporated milk, and heavy cream or Cool Whip to replace the tedious and time-consuming process of boiling down the milk. This recipe requires only a blender, a freezer, and a tiny bit of patience.

In a blender, combine the condensed milk, evaporated milk, cream, almonds, 1 teaspoon cardamom, and saffron and blend until smooth. Pour the mixture into a loaf pan and scatter the remaining ½ teaspoon cardamom and the chopped pistachios over the top. Cover and freeze overnight, then slice and serve.

Shrikhand

1 (32-ounce) container plain full-fat yogurt
 (not Greek; see Ingredient Note)

1 cup sugar

1 pinch saffron

1 tablespoon whole milk

1 teaspoon ground cardamom, divided

1 tablespoon chopped pistachios,
 for garnish (optional)

🌿 INGREDIENT NOTE

It is crucial to use the right kind of yogurt to achieve the proper texture. The yogurt shouldn't be grass-fed or Greek-style, nor should it contain additives like cornstarch. I use Dannon or Desi Natural Dahi from the Indian grocery store.

My mom makes the best shrikhand in the world. I truly have yet to encounter a better version than hers, even in India. I know I sound incredibly biased (and I am because my mom is a brilliant cook), but the luscious texture she can achieve with shrikhand is unrivaled.

Shrikhand is one of the simplest sweets: sweetened strained yogurt flavored with saffron and cardamom. Many people strain the yogurt overnight using a cheesecloth or resourceful setups like coffee filters and colanders. Then they mix in the sugar, saffron, and cardamom. This shrikhand is good. But my mom does two things to make it epic.

First, her straining technique, which involves bath towels, is quicker and more effective than using cheesecloth in the fridge overnight. My mom can strain the yogurt in only 1½ to 2 hours. Her second trick is whipping the shrikhand with a hand mixer or a stand mixer, until it creates beautiful smooth ribbons that cascade down the bowl.

My mom will often make a large batch of shrikhand before a party (where she will serve it with Puri, page 253, and Gujarati Kadhi, page 217), and stick it in the freezer until the big day. My dad, like clockwork, will always swipe some of the frozen shrikhand directly from the container; he swears it is even better frozen. If you manage to have leftover shrikhand—how this happens, I don't know—pipe it into a profiterole or use as frosting for a cardamom or vanilla cake.

Recipe continues

Shrikhand freezes incredibly well and can stay in an airtight container in the freezer for up to 3 months. Just thaw it in the fridge before you're ready to eat it. Or you could eat it frozen, like my dad.

You need to strain the yogurt to get the optimal texture for shrikhand. There are many ways you can do this, but I prefer this method from my mom: Take two (clean) large bath towels and fold them into quarters. Place one towel on a table or kitchen counter and top with two large sheets of paper towel. Empty the entire container of yogurt onto the paper towels. Place two more sheets of paper towel on top of the yogurt, followed by the other bath towel. Place a cast-iron skillet or other heavy object (at least 4 or 5 pounds) on top of the top towel. Let the yogurt drain for about 1½ hours. Both the paper towels and the bath towels should be damp at this point from absorbing the water. Once the yogurt is drained and has the texture of a fresh cheese, transfer it to a large bowl. Add the sugar.

In a small bowl, combine the saffron and milk and microwave for 15 seconds (or heat the milk gently on the stove and then mix in the saffron).

Add the saffron milk to the strained yogurt, along with ½ teaspoon cardamom. Using a stand mixer or hand mixer, whip the yogurt mixture until it is well combined, smooth, and the texture of a luxurious, thick frosting. Garnish with the remaining ½ teaspoon cardamom and the pistachios, if using.

Mango Cardamom Tres Leches Cake

CAKE

4 large eggs

1 cup whole milk

1 box yellow cake mix

½ cup (4 tablespoons; ½ stick) melted butter

1 tablespoon vanilla extract

1 teaspoon ground cardamom

MILK SOAK

1 (14-ounce) can sweetened condensed milk

1 (12-ounce) can evaporated milk

¼ cup whole milk

½ cup canned mango pulp or fresh mango puree

WHIPPED TOPPING

2 cups heavy cream, chilled

½ cup sugar

1 teaspoon vanilla extract

½ teaspoon ground cardamom (optional)

½ cup canned mango pulp or fresh mango puree

Fresh mango slices, for decoration (optional)

This recipe is inspired by a dessert on the menu at Himalaya, the beloved Indian-Pakistani restaurant in Houston, Texas, where a slice of tres leches arrives with a pool of mango sauce cascading down the side. The cake is one example of where the Mexican and Indian palates overlap and how they influence one another in America.

I wanted to take the mango flavor one step further and infuse it into the cake as well. "More mango, less problems" is essentially my life motto. I turned to canned mango pulp from the Indian grocery store (you could also use fresh mango puree, which would be less sweet) and tossed cardamom into the whipped cream to make it even more Indian. Most traditional tres leches recipes ask you to separate your eggs and fold the whipped egg whites into the batter to make an airy sponge. If I am being honest, I always find that to be too much work, so I turned to boxed cake mix (a trick I picked up on the internet) to make a one bowl cake that comes together quickly.

Preheat the oven to 350 degrees F. Spray a 9 x 13-inch baking pan with nonstick cooking spray or grease with butter and dust with a light layer of flour.

In a large bowl, crack in the eggs and gently whisk until the yolks combine with the eggs. Then add in the cake mix, milk, melted butter, vanilla extract, and ground cardamom and whisk until evenly combined and a thick batter forms. Pour the batter into the prepared pan and bake for 25 to 30 minutes, until the top is a nice toasty, golden brown and a toothpick inserted in the center comes out clean. Let the cake cool to room temperature.

In a large bowl, crack in the eggs and gently whisk until the yolks combine with the eggs. Then add in the cake mix, milk, melted butter, vanilla extract, and ground cardamom and whisk until evenly combined and a thick batter forms. Pour the batter into the prepared pan and bake for 25 to 30 minutes, until the top is a nice toasty, golden brown and a toothpick inserted in the center comes out clean. Let the cake cool to room temperature.

In a large measuring cup or small bowl, combine the sweetened condensed milk, evaporated milk, whole milk, and mango pulp. Stir to evenly combine. Using a toothpick, a small, thin knife, or a fork, poke several holes all over the cake. Make sure the holes go through to the bottom of the cake (you really want the milk soak to get into every nook and cranny). Slowly drizzle the milk soak over the cake. It might take a few minutes for the milk to be absorbed, so do it in batches, until the mixture is gone and the cake is soaked. Cover and refrigerate for at least 4 hours, or ideally overnight to allow the flavors to meld.

When you're ready to serve, make the whipped topping. Combine the cream, sugar, vanilla, and cardamom (if using) in a large bowl and use an electric hand mixer or a stand mixer to whip the cream until stiff peaks form. Spread the topping over the cake. Drizzle the mango pulp over the cake, then decorate with the fresh mango slices, if using. (Alternatively, you can fold the mango pulp into the whipped topping.) Cut into slices and serve. Or grab a fork and eat it straight from the pan—dishes, who needs them?

Masala Chai Basque Cheesecake

MASALA CHAI CREAM

1½ cups heavy cream

3 tablespoons loose black tea

4 whole cloves

2 cinnamon sticks *or* ½ teaspoon ground cinnamon

1 teaspoon ground cardamom

CHEESECAKE BASE

4 (8-ounce) blocks full-fat cream cheese, at room temperature

1½ cups sugar

5 large eggs, at room temperature

2 teaspoons vanilla extract

1 teaspoon salt

¼ cup all-purpose flour

MASALA WHIPPED CREAM

½ cup heavy cream, chilled

2 tablespoons sugar

¼ teaspoon salt

¼ teaspoon ground cardamom

¼ teaspoon ground cinnamon

¼ teaspoon ground ginger

Pinch flaky sea salt

Crumbled Parle-G cookies (optional; see Ingredient Note)

Basque cheesecake—known for its signature burnt exterior and lack of crust—has always reminded me of chhena poda, a dessert popular in the eastern Indian state of Odisha that is essentially sweetened fresh cheese, baked for several hours until it achieves the same caramelized appearance. They are both wonderfully thick desserts, but I am partial to Basque cheesecake simply because I love the tang of cream cheese. I wanted to create a version that tasted like a cup of masala chai. You may encounter desserts that are chai-spiced, but so few are actually chai-*flavored*, an important distinction. The slightly bitter tea notes mellow out the cheesecake so that it's not as sweet as a lot of other Indian desserts.

Preheat the oven to 425 degrees F. Line a 9-inch springform pan with 2 large sheets of parchment paper, crisscrossed so that there are no gaps. The parchment paper should extend up and above the top rim of the springform pan by a few inches. Place the lined springform pan on a rimmed baking sheet and set aside.

To make the masala chai cream, in a small saucepan, combine the cream, tea leaves, cloves, cinnamon, and cardamom and bring to a boil. Turn the heat down to a simmer let the flavors steep while simmering for 5 minutes, stirring constantly. The color of the cream when it's properly infused should be the same as your morning latte. Strain and let cool to room temperature. You should have about 1¼ cups of liquid.

Recipe continues

In a large bowl, combine the cream cheese and sugar. Using either a stand mixer or a handheld mixer, beat the mixture until very smooth. You want zero lumps. This should take at least 2 to 3 minutes. Add the eggs, one at a time, continuing to beat the mixture until smooth. Once the eggs are mixed in, add the masala chai cream, vanilla, and salt. Mix again. Sprinkle the flour over the batter and mix on low speed until evenly combined.

Pour the batter into the prepared pan and bake for 50 to 60 minutes. The cheesecake should puff up and the top will look dark, somewhat burnt, and perhaps even cracked. This is normal and the reason why this cheesecake has so much flavor. The center of the cake should be a little jiggly, but the edges should be set. Place the pan on a wire rack and let cool to room temperature. The cake will deflate! This is also normal, and something you want to happen. Let the cake fully cool. It's best if you let it chill in the fridge overnight.

Before serving, make the masala whipped cream. Combine the cold cream, sugar, salt, cardamom, cinnamon, and ginger in a large bowl and beat using a stand mixer or handheld mixer on medium-high speed until the cream is a cloud-like consistency. Dollop on top of the cheesecake and scatter with cookie crumbs, if using. (But know it's always better with cookies.)

Almond Katli

4 cups almond flour

3 cups powdered sugar

2 cups milk powder

1 tablespoon ground cardamom

2 pinches saffron

¾ cup whole milk, divided

2 teaspoons ghee

Crushed pistachios, edible rose petals,
   edible silver foil, for garnish (optional)

◉ SERVING NOTE

Traditionally, kaju katli is garnished with sheets of edible silver foil, which adds zero flavor but maximum vibes. I decorate my almond katli with edible rose petals and crushed pistachios, but the katli is also delicious without any embellishments.

✳ FREEZER NOTE

Almond katli freezes well. Layer the pieces between pieces of parchment or wax paper in an airtight container. Thaw at room temperature before serving.

If I were a professor teaching a course called Indian Sweets 101, my very first class would probably be about kaju katli. The cashew-based burfi is widely beloved and sold everywhere. It's relatively simple to make at home, It involves grinding cashews into a fine powder, which can be tricky, so the easier method is to make almond katli instead. It's a brilliant trick I learned from my mom, who started making almond katli after noticing the prevalence of almond flour at supermarkets. The microwave makes quick work of this recipe, and it's perfect for when you need a last-second sweet.

In a large microwave-safe bowl, whisk together the almond flour, powdered sugar, milk powder, and cardamom.

In a small microwave-safe bowl, microwave the saffron for 25 seconds, then crush the dried-out saffron strands with your fingers back into the bowl. Add ¼ cup milk to the bowl and microwave for another 20 seconds, then swirl the milk around the bowl. It should be sunshine-y yellow (this trick allows you to use less saffron but extract maximum flavor and color). Pour the saffron milk into the almond flour mixture and stir until well combined. The dough will be dry and powdery.

Microwave the dough, uncovered, for 1½ minutes. Add another ¼ cup milk, stir well, and microwave the dough for another minute. Repeat this step once more with the remaining ¼ cup milk. The dough should easily clump together. Add the ghee, microwave for another minute, and stir with a spoon until the mixture comes together into a dough that is very smooth and a little glossy.

Line a rimmed baking sheet with parchment paper and place the dough on the sheet. Using a flat-bottomed bowl greased with ghee, or with another piece of parchment paper, spread the dough across the sheet into an even layer, no more than ¼ inch thick. Decorate with crushed pistachios, rose petals, and edible silver foil, if using. Cut the katli into diamond-shaped pieces.

ALMOND KATLI
(PAGE 299)

NUTELLA BURFI

Nutella Burfi

Crushed hazelnuts or sliced
    almonds, for topping
¼ cup ghee or unsalted butter
1 (14-ounce) can sweetened
    condensed milk
¾ cup Nutella
1½ cups nonfat milk powder

🍲 STORAGE NOTE

I wouldn't freeze these. They last in an air-tight container in the fridge for 3 days or so before they start drying out.

Perhaps the most basic category of Indian desserts are burfi, dense and fudge-like treats made from khoya (slow-cooked milk), sugar, and other flavorings. One of my favorite flavors growing up was chocolate burfi, which gets its flavor from the addition of cocoa powder and is sold at Indian grocers and sweet shops across the country. Over the years, I'd heard of wild variations from cookies and cream burfi to Snickers burfi, but I hadn't come across Nutella burfi yet—and I figured that if chocolate burfi works so well, there is no reason a chocolate-hazelnut burfi shouldn't be delicious, too. I use a shortcut, taught to me by my mother (and common in burfi-making), where I swap milk powder for the khoya. The key is to roast the milk powder in a pan to cook out the powdery flavor before you add the other ingredients.

Line an 8 x 8–inch baking pan with parchment paper and leave 1 inch hanging over the edges. Spread an even layer of hazelnuts on the parchment and set aside.

Melt the ghee in a large nonstick skillet over medium heat. Add the condensed milk and Nutella and give it a stir. Add the milk powder and stir continuously for 3 to 5 minutes, until the mixture is well combined and starts pulling away from the sides of the pan. Immediately remove the pan from the heat.

Pour the Nutella mixture over the nuts in the pan. Press the mixture evenly across the pan using another sheet of parchment paper. Let it cool, then lift the burfi out of the pan using the parchment paper and place on flat surface. Lightly oil a sharp knife and use it to cut the burfi into 25 squares. Flip the squares over and serve. Refrigerate if not serving immediately.

Jaggery and Fennel Rice Krispie Treats

½ cup or 4 tablespoons unsalted butter

½ cup ghee

½ cup packed jaggery

2 (12-ounce) bags marshmallows

1 (12-ounce) box crispy rice cereal

1 cup candy-coated fennel seeds
   (also sold as fennel candy)

1 teaspoon flaky sea salt

❦ INGREDIENT NOTE

If you are vegetarian or you don't eat gelatin, you can sub in vegan marshmallows (I like Dandies brand). Just keep in mind that vegan marshmallows look lumpier when they've melted down, so don't be alarmed. If you can't find jaggery, it's okay to use brown sugar instead, but I like the caramel notes jaggery brings to the recipe.

❄ FREEZER NOTE

The treats keeps well in an airtight container at room temperature for up to 5 days. Or you can freeze them, with parchment papers between layers, for up to 3 months.

There's a snack sold at most Indian stores that is essentially puffed rice combined with melted jaggery, shaped into ornament-sized balls. It's known as murmura laddu or pori urundai (depending on which part of India your family is from), and it's the perfect treat, minus one thing: I always wished the murmura laddu had the satisfyingly gooey stretch of a good Rice Krispie treat. So I combined my favorite elements of both snacks into one super snack. I upgraded the flavor and texture (and aesthetics!) by adding those beloved colorful candied fennel seeds often served after dinner on the way out of any Indian restaurant. They are a must in this recipe and can be purchased online or at any Indian grocery. Also keep in mind that these treats are extra thick, with some serious height. Halve the recipe if you prefer thinner treats.

Line a 9 x 13-inch baking pan with parchment paper.

Melt the butter and ghee in a large pot over medium heat. Add the jaggery and stir until melted, 2 to 3 minutes. Add the marshmallows and turn the heat down to low. Let the marshmallows melt and become gooey, 4 to 5 minutes, stirring occasionally. The final texture should be like a thick, creamy face moisturizer. It's normal to see streaks of jaggery in the marshmallow. Turn off the heat and stir in the cereal until everything is evenly coated, then mix in the candied fennel.

Pour the cereal mixture into the prepared pan. Press into an even layer using another piece of parchment paper. Top with the flaky sea salt, then let cool and harden, at least 1 hour. Cut into squares and serve.

Menu Ideas

Thanksgiving

Masala Deviled Eggs (page 73)

Endive and Paneer Salad with Tamarind Chutney Vinaigrette (page 234)

Green Bean Thoran (page 227)

Tadka Focaccia (page 258)

Makhani Mac and Cheese (page 162)

Biryani Baked in a Squash (page 159)

Cucumber Raita (page 64)

Mango Pie (page 282)

Easy Freezer Kulfi (page 290)

Pizza Party

Tandoori Chicken Wings (page 86)

Amchur Ranch Salad with Crispy Chickpeas (page 237)

Achari Paneer Pizza (page 136)

Cheesy Masala Corn Pizza (page 145)

Green Chutney Pizza (page 147)

Jaggery and Fennel Rice Krispie Treats (page 302)

Indo-Chinese Lunch

Cauliflower Manchurian (page 240)

Hakka Noodles (page 165)

Chili Paneer Dumplings (page 213)

Bobalooda (page 271)

Sunday Brunch

Shahi Tukda French Toast (page 29)

Saag Paneer Frittata (page 26)

Saffron Chia Seed Pudding (page 27)

Masala Smashed Potatoes (page 233)

Dad's Adu Ka Jaddu Masala Chai (page 71)

Shikanji Pimm's Cup (page 279)

Dosa Dinner

Dosa Masala (page 124)

Chile Cheese Dosas (page 123)

Garlic Bread Dosas (page 123)

Sambar (page 131)

Coconut Chutney (page 56)

Gunpowder Chutney (page 57)

Afternoon Tea

Dad's Adu Ka Jaddu Masala Chai (page 71)

Saffron Gin and Tonic (page 278)

Chutney Tea Sandwiches (page 97)

Cocktail Pizza Samosas (page 120)

Breakfast Cereal Chevvdo (page 74)

Kale Pakoras (page 83)

Nutella Burfi (page 301)

Game Day

Tandoori Chicken Wings (page 86)

Jalapeño Popper Samosas (page 116)

Naan Pizza (page 149)

Masala Poutine (page 78)

Rajma Nachos (page 174)

Aloo Paratha Quesadillas (page 177)

Lasagna Night

Masala Roasted Garlic Bread (page 261)

Endive and Paneer Salad with Tamarind
   Chutney Vinaigrette (page 234)

Saag Paneer Lasagna (page 169)

Malai Broccoli (page 230)

Masala Chai Basque Cheesecake (page 297)

Diwali Party

Peanut Chaat (page 87)

Tortilla Papdi Chaat (page 90)

Samosa Pinwheels (page 117)

Shrimp Moilee (page 186)

Paneer Tikka Masala (page 185)

Spinach Jeera Rice (page 152)

Simple Parathas (page 244)

Gulab Jamun (page 285)

Shikanji Pimm's Cup (page 279)

Summer Cookout

Masala Veggie Burgers (page 98)

Bombay Grill Sandwich (page 110)

Lemon Seviyan (page 168)

Classic Kachumber (page 226)

Masala Smashed Potatoes (page 233)

Mango Pie (page 282)

Jaggery and Fennel Rice Krispie Treats
   (page 302)

Tamarind Chutney Margaritas
   (page 275)

Pani Puri Mojitos (page 273)

Suggested Further Reading

My most prized possession might be my collection of South Asian cookbooks. They take up several shelves in my apartment, and I am always on the hunt for books to help expand my collection. Of the books that I own, there's a stack that I return to over and over again when I am looking for background information or inspiration. Here are some of my favorites:

One Spice, Two Spice by Floyd Cardoz

Made in India by Meera Sodha

Classic Indian Cooking by Julie Sahni

Vegetarian India by Madhur Jaffrey

An Invitation to Indian Cooking by Madhur Jaffrey

Indian-ish by Priya Krishna

Plant-Based India by Sheil Shukla

Asma's Indian Kitchen by Asma Khan

On the Curry Trail by Raghavan Iyer

Curry: A Tale of Cooks and Conquerors by Lizzie Collingham

Chaat by Maneet Chauhan

Kricket: An Indian-Inspired Cookbook by Will Bowlby

Acknowledgments

I always love flipping to the back of cookbooks to read the author's acknowledgments. It's a testament to the fact that no cookbook is truly a solo project. Here are mine:

Mom: I will always be the luckiest person on this planet because you are my mother. I am in awe at the strength with which you walk through this world, and yet, there is nothing that a hug from you cannot fix. Everyone says their mom is the best cook, but you really are the best cook. (Your knife skills alone are deeply impressive.) Thank you for being patient with me as I made you stop every two seconds to measure out ingredients while you were cooking and for answering a million annoying questions. You really just are the best mom. I love you.

Dad: Thank you for my hair genes. And for the unconditional love that you and mom give me, even though at the time of writing this, I am 32, unmarried, not a doctor, and have a million big insane dreams that deviate from any path of safety or stability you guys have ever known. Thank you for always encouraging me. I love you.

Jainil: The day you were born was the happiest day of my life. I could not ask for a sweeter little brother. Thank you for helping to wash dishes and test recipes when you could, for telling me that things always sounded delicious, and for being excited about my book even in the moments I was plagued with self-doubt. I love you.

To Melanie Tortoroli: Thank you for being a dream editor and collaborator. Writing a book is a daunting process, but your encouraging notes, thoughtful edits, and boundless excitement made this process a joyful one. Your belief in me means everything.

To David Black: I'm pretty sure there is nothing I can't do with you in my corner. You are one hell of an agent, and your guidance, patience, and relentlessness have been invaluable through this whole journey. I appreciate how you always keep it real. Thank you for believing in me and my vision.

To Aubrie Pick: From the day I started writing the proposal for this book, I had no other photographer in mind but you. All of our plotting really paid off. You were a true creative and a total badass. I am so lucky to have had the honor of getting to collaborate with you and to watch you weave your magic. I am even luckier to have been able to call you my friend. This shoot will forever be one of my fondest memories. I miss you, but I see you everywhere in these pages. Fuck cancer.

To Carrie Ann Purcell: Thank you for making all the food in this book look so good, and for dealing with the chaos of Indian grocery stores, and the days my family came to set. Your patience and organizational skills are unrivaled.

To Nissa Quanstrom: Thank you for sourcing such an immense selection of props. The brief you were given was a challenging one, but you showed up with so many beautiful and playful options.

To Badal Patel: From the moment I signed my book deal, I knew I wanted to have you involved in the project. Your aesthetic and design sense are incredible and I knew if someone could help make this book feel equal parts Indian and American, it would be you.

To the over 100 people who volunteered to test recipes from this book—whether you know me personally or not: I really appreciate your time and your feedback! It has been invaluable.

To Priya Krishna, Sonia Chopra, and Tejal Rao: I cannot imagine life without the three of you. I will never be able to thank you enough for the endless advice, support, encouragement, and gut checks you have provided me over the years. I deeply admire each of you and am so thankful I get to go through life with your friendships. Sambar Squad forever.

To Bill Addison: I hope no one can ever hack into our voice notes to each other. Thank you for always being there, for always letting me vent, and for eating at the bar at Quarter Sheets with me whenever things got too stressful. I cannot wait for your future book.

To Radha Mistry, Aishwarya Iyer, Disha Mahendro, and Zarna Surti: Kitty Party, thank you for the endless hugs and notes of encouragement. For always being around to talk through things with me, or willing to give your thoughtful feedback. Thank you for reminding me to rest, the couch hangs, and the belly laughs. Los Angeles feels like home, largely because of the four of you.

To my cousins Sahil, Sunny, Ronak, and Sejal: Thank you for showing up to set, for hand modeling, and for saying the food is great and then actually eating all of it.

To Jolly Mami: You are the best aunt. Thank you for letting me raid your house for props and for hand modeling.

To Hunter Lewis and Mel Hansche: Thank you for not only creating space for me to be able to write this book while working a truly insane (and incredible) job at F&W, but also encouraging me to do it. You are the best bosses I have ever had.

To Samin Nosrat: Thank you for your invaluable advice during this process. You did not have to spend so many hours on the phone with me, and I deeply appreciate it.

To Eric Kim: Thank you for your generosity during the proposal process. I appreciate everything you shared with me. It helped me put my own proposal together.

To my neighbors Minna, Jori, Kayleigh, and Gabe: Thank you for eating endless recipe tests, and running up so many packages for me.

To Something & Nothing, Spindrift, and Topo Chico: I appreciate you for making the ridiculous amounts of seltzer I consumed while writing this book.

To Carrie Beyer and Vanessa Solis: This shoot was fast and furious and would not have been possible without both of your incredible skills as an assistant food stylist and assistant photographer, respectively. Thank you for your energy and positive attitude, even on the longest of days.

To the W. W. Norton Team: This book wouldn't exist without your hard work and dedication. Thank you for caring about every little detail. A special shoutout to Allison Chi for all your guidance with the visuals of this book.

And finally, I want to thank me. In the iconic words of Snoop Dogg: "I wanna thank me for believing in me. I wanna thank me for doing all this hard work . . . I wanna thank me for never quitting." Writing a book, especially one that is so personal and yet for the culture, while working my insanely demanding and busy full-time job, almost broke me at times. There was a lot of writing until 3 a.m., or sprints of developing two or three recipes in one day, more dishes to wash than I care to remember, and plenty of self-doubt along the way. I am proud that I brought it across the finish line. I would be honored if this book can find a place on your shelves.

Index

Note: Page references in *italics* indicate photographs.

KHUSHBU SHAH

is a food writer and journalist who resides in Los Angeles, California. She was most recently the restaurant editor at *Food & Wine* magazine, where she crisscrossed the United States several times over on the hunt for the country's best new chefs. She is the youngest person and the only person of color to ever hold that title. You can also find her work in the *New York Times*, *Washington Post*, *GQ*, *Eater*, and more. Additionally, her writing has been featured in the *Best American Food Writing* anthologies, and she has made appearances on television shows like *Ugly Delicious*. Khushbu grew up in Michigan, where her immigrant parents raised her with a deep appreciation for spices and good fruit. This is her debut cookbook.